COOKING
— FOR THE —
MAN CAVE

WHAT TO EAT WHEN YOU'RE KICKING BACK WITH FAMILY & FRIENDS

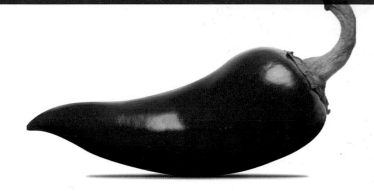

Edited by Paul McGahren

FOX CHAPEL
PUBLISHING

FOOD IS SERIOUS.* COOKING IS A GAME.** PLAY TO WIN.

Cook proudly.

Cook generously.

Cook manly.

HERE'S THE PLAYBOOK.

*…ly delicious. And necessary. You know this. You're thinking about it right now.
**An incredible one. It has timers, temperature extremes, physicality, strategy…and obligatory after-game eats.

© 2016 by Fox Chapel Publishing Company, Inc., East Petersburg, PA.

Recipe selection, design, and book design © Fox Chapel Publishing.
Recipes and photography © G&R Publishing DBA CQ Products.

Edited by Paul McGahren.

ISBN 978-1-56523-892-3

Library of Congress Cataloging-in-Publication Data

Names: McGahren, Paul, editor. | Fox Chapel Publishing.
Title: Cooking for the man cave / edited by Paul McGahren.
Description: Second edition. | East Petersburg, Pennsylvania : Fox Chapel Publishing, [2016] | Includes index.
Identifiers: LCCN 2015044316 | ISBN 9781565238923
Subjects: LCSH: Cooking. | Cooking, American. | Recreation rooms. | Male friendship.
Classification: LCC TX652 .C656 2016 | DDC 641.5973--dc23
LC record available at http://lccn.loc.gov/2015044316

To learn more about the other great books from Fox Chapel Publishing, or to find a retailer near you, call toll-free 800-457-9112 or visit us at *www.FoxChapelPublishing.com*.

Note to Authors: We are always looking for talented authors to write new books. Please send a brief letter describing your idea to Acquisition Editor, 1970 Broad Street, East Petersburg, PA 17520.

Printed in China
First printing

Introduction

Mothers cook with love. **MEN COOK WITH ATTITUDE:** what they want, when they want, for friends. *Spectacularly.*

★ ★ ★ ★ ★

Man Cave cooking isn't about physical location.

★ ★ ★ ★ ★

It's about partying in the backyard with the neighborhood guys you shoveled snow with a few months ago.

★ ★ ★ ★ ★

It's about grilling in the park with your teammates after you won the semifinal.

★ ★ ★ ★ ★

It's about gathering around the campfire with your brothers after a long day's paddle on the Allagash River.

★ ★ ★ ★ ★

It's about tailgating with your college pals before the first game of the season.

★ ★ ★ ★ ★

It's about celebrating your best friend's wedding with the rest of the groomsmen in your tricked-out den.

★ ★ ★ ★ ★

It's about frying the biggest turkey you can find and then eating every shred of it.

★ ★ ★ ★ ★

IT'S ABOUT… well no, it isn't about the meal you eat right after you summit Mount Everest. That's probably some nasty freeze-dried M.R.E. But apart from Mount Everest, if it's masculine and involves friends and fun, it almost certainly calls for some **MAN CAVE COOKING.**

That's where this book comes in. Consider it your personal coach to creating swaggeringly good food—and, not incidentally, a staggeringly good time. It's a cool coach, prone to awesomeness and stressing on only the really important things, such as how to use your turkey fryer without requiring the services of the fire department or ambulance crews. Or which sporting events you really need to see in person at least once.

The chapters cover cooking in the turkey fryer, on the grill, and in the kitchen, with further divisions to help you find the perfect main dish, sides, snack, or dessert. There are, notably, lots of meat recipes and lots of recipes for cooking with beer. But one food does not a meal make, so be sure to pay attention to the smaller dishes too. They're supporting actors, of sorts—and as fully capable of brilliance as the stars.

★ ★ ★ ★ ★

NEED STEAK? It's here.

NEED BEER~CAN CHICKEN? It's here.

NEED FRIED DILL PICKLES? It's here.

NEED GERMAN POTATO SALAD? It's here.

NEED BEER CHEESE SAUSAGE SOUP? It's here.

BROWSE AND BE INSPIRED. Try them all.

★ ★ ★ ★ ★

As you're browsing, you'll notice a wealth of tips scattered liberally among the recipes. They cover food, trivia, and other vital topics for your enjoyment and edification. Next time things get a little slow, pull this out and set the guys loose on it. In less time than it took Dale Earnhardt to gun that motor, you'll have a list of requested recipes and a couple of lively debates.

★ ★ ★ ★ ★ ★ ★ ★ ★ ★ ★ ★ ★ ★ ★

GREAT THINGS HAPPEN WHEN A MAN COOKS IN HIS CAVE.

GO ON AND HAVE A GO AT THEM.

★ ★ ★ ★ ★ ★ ★ ★ ★ ★ ★ ★ ★ ★

TABLE OF CONTENTS

Other Meats

Sides

Boiled

Camp or Kitchen

Sweets

CHAPTER 2: KING OF THE GRILL

Meats

Sides

CHAPTER 3: MAN OF THE KITCHEN 80

Skillet

Slow Cooker

Main Dishes

Sides

Salads

1

Lord of the Fryer

Deep~frying is the Evel Knievel of cooking techniques.

Done right, the results are irresistible. Done wrong, the damage is horrifying. The combination of drama and danger makes it a can't-miss spectacle, and when you pull out those outrageously good eats, the smell may well inspire people to crash your party.

The trick is, of course, doing it right. Incinerate anyone or anything—including the food—and you'll go from chow champ to vittle villain. The rules for safety are on page 16 under the heading "Deep Frying: Don't be the Turkey." Ignore them at your peril. Follow them as you would a drill sergeant's shouts and you'll be fine.

Okay, obeying all safety rules all the time. Good. The success rules are fewer and more fun:

♠ Be safe.

♥ Use our blueprints for deliciousness.

♣ Eat as soon as the food is cool enough, and in one sitting. "Leftover" and "deep-fried" are incompatible concepts.

♦ Invite a bunch of friends to share the awesomeness. Big fryers call for big parties. Plus—gotta say it—your arteries will thank you.

ON TO AWESOMENESS!

Turkey fryers are the biggest, baddest deep fryers out there, so the bulk of this chapter focuses on them. Obviously you expect to use them on turkey, so we'll start with that, and then move on to an array of other deep-fried meats, side dishes, and desserts that will make your salivary glands ache. Turkey fryers can also produce some memorable meals that involve neither turkey nor deep-frying, so we threw in a couple of those for variety. And some non-turkey-fryer-but-fried dishes on a smaller scale round out the chapter, for use in your kitchen or on a camping trip.

HOW TO CARVE A TURKEY

1. Allow the turkey to rest at least 15 minutes before carving. The turkey can rest up to half an hour, if desired.

2. Get the right carving utensils. A long-pronged fork and a long sharp knife work the best.

3. Place turkey on a large cutting board, breast side up. Hold the turkey with the fork and run the sharp knife down the breastbone on each side of the turkey.

4. Remove the entire breast from the turkey and slice the breast meat crosswise to desired thickness.

5. Using a kitchen towel, hold onto the end of one drumstick with one hand and run the knife between the drumstick and the body of the turkey. Cut through the meat to the joint and twist slightly to remove the drumstick.

6. Remove each wing by cutting between the wing and the frame of the turkey.

7. Present turkey by fanning breast slices out on a serving platter. Place drumsticks and wings on the platter as well. Serve and enjoy!

DEEP-FRYING: DON'T BE THE TURKEY

♠ Read and follow all manufacturer's instructions for your turkey fryer and propane tank.

♥ Never use a turkey fryer indoors, in a garage, under a structure attached to a building, or on a wooden deck. Frying a turkey over concrete can stain the concrete, so it is best to find a level dirt or grass area.

♣ Be sure the frying area is open and away from buildings, trees, shrubs, children, and pets.

♦ Keep at least 2 feet of space between the propane tank and the fryer burner. Make sure any wind blows the heat of the fryer away from the gas tank, not toward it.

♠ Center the fryer over the burner.

♥ Use only oil with a high smoke point. Peanut, canola, and safflower oils are good choices.

IMPORTANT

♣ To determine the correct amount of oil, place the turkey in the fryer (before adding any seasonings) and fill the pot with water until the turkey is covered. Remove turkey and measure the amount of water in the fryer. Use the corresponding amount of oil when frying the turkey. Dry the fryer thoroughly of all water before adding oil or storing.

♦ Completely thaw and dry the food before cooking. Partially frozen or wet foods can produce excessive splattering when added to hot oil. The USDA recommends 24 hours of thaw time in a refrigerator for each 4 to 5 pounds of turkey meat.

♠ Immediately wash hands, utensils, equipment, gloves, and any surfaces that have come in contact with a raw turkey or other raw meat.

♥ Wear oven mitts or gloves, long sleeves, and glasses to prevent burns caused by splattering oil. A face shield and safety glasses are a good idea, too.

♣ Keep a fire extinguisher nearby. A bucket of sand would not be amiss.

♦ Never leave the turkey fryer unattended. Keep careful watch throughout the cooking process.

♠ If the oil begins to smoke, immediately turn off the gas.

♥ If a grease fire occurs, immediately turn off the gas and cover the pot with a lid. Call 911. Do not attempt to extinguish the fire with water.

♣ Lower food into the fryer s-l-o-w-l-y and raise it out the same way. For whole turkeys and other unwieldy and heavy foods it's best to have an assistant—just make sure your helper is also dressed protectively.

♦ Let hot oil cool completely before transferring to storage containers or disposing. Cooled oil can be transferred to empty, clean milk jugs or buckets and stored in a refrigerator. Once oil has been used for cooking, it should be treated as a meat product and kept cool in a refrigerator. If properly stored, oil can be safely used up to three times. Signs of oil deterioration include foaming, darkening, and excessive smoking.

TURKEY-FRYING BASICS Makes 12 servings

INGREDIENTS
- 10 to 12 lb. whole turkey, not self-basting, fresh or thoroughly thawed
- 4 to 5 gallons peanut oil (see Note 1 on page 17)

PREPARATION
Remove any plastic bags or pop-up timer from turkey. Remove giblets and neck from turkey and rinse turkey in cold water. Use paper towels to thoroughly dry both outside and inside cavity of turkey. Cut the wing tips from the turkey, as well as small tail, as they may get caught in the fryer basket. Add measured amount of peanut oil to a 7 to 10 gallon fryer pot. Set fryer to medium-high setting and heat oil until the deep-fry thermometer reaches 375°F; it should take about 40+ minutes. Meanwhile, place turkey in the turkey fryer basket or on the rack, neck down. Slowly lower turkey into the oil (see Note 9 on page 17). Because of frothing caused by the moisture from the turkey, the level of the oil will rise, but will stabilize in about 1 minute. Immediately check the oil temperature and increase the

flame so the oil temperature is maintained at 350°. If the oil temperature drops to 340° or below, oil will begin to seep into the turkey. Fry turkey for about 3 to 4 minutes per pound, or about 35 to 42 minutes for a 10 to 12 pound turkey. Be sure to stay near the cooker, as the heat must be closely regulated. Using a meat thermometer, check the temperature of the breast or thigh. When the breast has been cooked to 170° F or the thigh has been cooked to 180° F, carefully remove the turkey from the hot oil and turn off the fryer. Allow the turkey to drain for a few minutes. Remove turkey from rack and place on a serving platter. Allow turkey to rest for about 20 minutes before carving. Let hot oil cool completely before transferring to storage containers or disposing (see Note 10 on page 17).

DEEP-FRIED TURKEY MADE EASY

INGREDIENTS
- Salt
- Lemon juice
- Hot pepper sauce
- Lemon wedges for garnish

PREPARATION
Follow Turkey-Frying Basics, above. After carving, sprinkle turkey generously with salt and lemon juice. Serve with hot pepper sauce on the side. Garnish with fresh lemon wedges.

MAPLE PECAN GLAZED DEEP-FRIED TURKEY

INGREDIENTS
- ¼ C. maple syrup
- 3 T. butter
- 2 T. Dijon mustard
- 2 T. whiskey
- ¼ C. finely chopped pecans, toasted*
- Salt and pepper to taste

PREPARATION
Follow Turkey-Frying Basics, page 18. While turkey is frying, combine maple syrup, butter, Dijon mustard, whiskey, and chopped toasted pecans in a medium saucepan over medium heat. Bring mixture to a boil, stirring frequently. Reduce heat and let simmer for 2 to 3 minutes. After turkey has drained for a few minutes, spoon glaze over hot turkey. Allow turkey to rest for about 15 more minutes before carving. Season with salt and pepper.

*To toast, place finely chopped pecans in a single layer on a baking sheet. Bake at 350° for approximately 10 minutes or until pecans are golden brown.

ONION STUFFED DEEP-FRIED TURKEY WITH HONEY BEER SAUCE

INGREDIENTS

- 1 medium yellow onion, cut into ¼" slices
- 2 T. beer
- 2 T. honey
- 2 T. Dijon mustard
- 1 tsp. fresh chopped thyme

PREPARATION

Follow Turkey-Frying Basics, page 18. Loosen skin over breast area of turkey by carefully slipping fingers between skin and meat. Gently lift the skin and slide onion slices under the skin. While turkey is frying combine beer, honey, Dijon mustard, and fresh chopped thyme in a small bowl. Mix well. After turkey has drained for a few minutes, spoon honey and beer mixture over hot turkey. Allow turkey to rest for about 15 more minutes before carving.

THE ORIGINAL

INGREDIENTS

- ½ (16 oz.) bottle Italian dressing
- 2 T. Worcestershire sauce
- Hot sauce to taste
- ¼ C. salt
- 2 T. pepper
- 1 T. cayenne pepper
- 1 T. onion powder
- 1 T. garlic powder
- 1 T. celery salt
- ½ C. water

PREPARATION

Follow Turkey-Frying Basics, page 18. In a blender or food processor, combine Italian dressing, Worcestershire sauce, hot sauce, salt, pepper, cayenne pepper, onion powder, garlic powder, celery salt, and water. Blend for 2 to 3 minutes until seasonings are liquefied. Place turkey in a large roasting pan. Use a poultry injector to inject marinade two to three times on each side of the breast and upper thighs. If desired, inject any additional marinade into meaty parts of turkey.

SOUTHERN DEEP-FRIED TURKEY

INGREDIENTS
- ⅔ C. vinaigrette dressing
- ⅓ C. dry sherry
- 2 tsp. lemon pepper seasoning salt
- 1 tsp. garlic powder
- 1 tsp. onion powder
- 1 tsp. cayenne pepper

PREPARATION
Follow Turkey-Frying Basics, page 18. In a small bowl, combine vinaigrette, dry sherry, lemon pepper seasoning salt, garlic powder, onion powder, and cayenne pepper. Mix until well blended and strain marinade through a fine-hole sieve or cheesecloth. Place turkey in a large roasting pan. Use a poultry injector to inject marinade two to three times on each side of the breast and upper thighs. If desired, inject any additional marinade into meaty parts of turkey.

SPICY ITALIAN DEEP-FRIED TURKEY

INGREDIENTS
- 1 C. Italian dressing, strained
- 1 C. white wine
- 1 (26 oz.) box free-flowing salt
- 3 T. pepper
- ¼ C. cayenne pepper
- 2 T. garlic powder
- 2 T. chili powder

PREPARATION
Follow Turkey-Frying Basics, page 18. In a small bowl, combine strained Italian dressing and white wine. In a separate bowl, combine salt, pepper, cayenne pepper, garlic powder, and chili powder. Mix until well blended and sprinkle half of the salt mixture over the Italian dressing mixture. Stir thoroughly and constantly so the dressing and wine do not separate. Place turkey in a large roasting pan and, using a poultry injector, season the turkey by injecting marinade two to three times on each side of the breast and upper thighs. Rub remaining half of the salt mixture over the outside and inside cavity of turkey. Cover roasting pan and turkey with a plastic bag and place overnight in refrigerator.

DOUBLE SPICY DEEP-FRIED TURKEY

INGREDIENTS
- ½ C. liquid garlic
- ½ C. liquid onion
- ½ C. liquid celery
- 1 T. cayenne pepper
- 2 T. salt
- 2 T. Tabasco sauce
- 2 T. liquid crab boil or 1 tsp. Old Bay seasoning

PREPARATION
Follow Turkey-Frying Basics, page 18. To make marinade, combine liquid garlic, liquid onion, liquid celery, cayenne pepper, salt, Tabasco sauce, and liquid crab boil in a medium frying pan over medium-high heat. Sauté until cayenne pepper and salt are completely dissolved. Place turkey in a large roasting pan. Use a poultry injector to inject marinade two to three times on each side of the breast and upper thighs. If desired, inject any additional marinade into meaty parts of turkey.

CAJUN DEEP-FRIED TURKEY

INGREDIENTS

- ½ C. kosher salt
- 3 T. onion powder
- 3 T. pepper
- 3 T. white pepper
- 2 T. sweet basil
- 2 tsp. ground bay leaves
- 1 T. cayenne pepper
- 2 tsp. file powder
- 3 T. garlic powder
- 1½ T. paprika

PREPARATION

Follow Turkey-Frying Basics, page 18. In a small bowl, combine salt, onion powder, pepper, white pepper, sweet basil, ground bay leaves, cayenne pepper, file powder, garlic powder, and paprika. Mix until well blended. For a 10 to 12 pound turkey, use ½ to ⅔ cup of the mixture as a rub. The remaining rub can be stored in an airtight jar for several months. Place turkey in a large roasting pan and rub seasoning over the outside and inside cavity of turkey. Cover roasting pan and place in refrigerator overnight.

GINGER & ROSEMARY DEEP-FRIED TURKEY

INGREDIENTS

- ¼ C. fresh minced garlic
- 2 T. kosher salt
- 2 tsp. pepper
- ¼ C. fresh gingerroot, peeled and sliced
- 2 T. fresh rosemary, crushed
- 6 cloves garlic, peeled

PREPARATION

Follow Turkey-Frying Basics, page 18. In a small bowl, combine minced garlic, salt, and pepper. Mix until well blended. Fill cavity of turkey with sliced gingerroot, crushed rosemary, and garlic cloves. Place turkey in a large roasting pan and rub minced garlic seasoning over both inside and outside of turkey. Cover roasting pan and place in refrigerator for 1 hour. Then, remove ginger, rosemary, and garlic from turkey cavity and place turkey in the turkey fryer basket or on the rack, neck down.

LOUISIANA FRIED TURKEY BREAST Makes 6 servings

INGREDIENTS

- 1 T. kosher salt
- ¼ tsp. pepper
- 1 T. onion powder
- 1½ tsp. garlic powder
- 1 tsp. cayenne pepper
- 1 (3½ to 4 lb.) turkey breast, not self-basting
- 2 to 3 gallons peanut oil (see Note 1 on page 17)

PREPARATION

In a small bowl, combine kosher salt, pepper, onion powder, garlic powder, and cayenne pepper. Stir until seasonings are fully combined. Rinse turkey breast completely in cold water. Use paper towels to thoroughly dry both outside and inside of turkey breast. Rub seasoning mixture to coat all surfaces of the turkey breast. Place turkey breast in the turkey fryer basket or on the rack, neck side down. Add measured amount of peanut oil to a 7 to 10 gallon fryer pot (see Note 1 on page 17). Set fryer to medium-high setting and heat oil until the deep-fry thermometer reaches 375°F; it should take about 30+ minutes. Slowly lower turkey breast into the oil (see Note 9 on page 17). Because of frothing caused by the moisture from the turkey breast, the level of the oil will rise but will stabilize in about 1 minute. Immediately check the oil temperature and increase the flame so the oil temperature is maintained at 350°. If the oil temperature drops to 340° or below, oil will begin to seep into the turkey. Fry turkey for about 4 to 5 minutes per pound, or about 15 to 20 minutes for a 3½ to 4 pound turkey breast. Using a meat thermometer, check the temperature of the breast. When the breast has been cooked to 170° F, carefully remove the turkey breast from the hot oil and turn off the fryer. Allow the breast to drain for a few minutes. Remove turkey breast from rack and place on a serving platter. Allow turkey breast to rest for about 15 minutes before carving.

★★★★ MAN CAVE TIP ★★★★

THE NEED FOR SPEED

Want another great reason to fry a turkey? It's incredibly fast. Roasting a turkey takes roughly 20 minutes per pound; frying takes only about 3 minutes per pound. That Thanksgiving Day 15-pounder will hog up your stove for more than 4 hours, while the same turkey will be fried to moist perfection in 45 minutes. Plus, you get to hang out in the yard while you enjoy a cold one and argue sports. (Just remember...do not fry drunk.)

SPICY FRIED CHICKEN Makes 16 servings

INGREDIENTS

- Frying oil
- 4 (3 lb.) whole chickens
- 2 qt. buttermilk
- ¼ C. Tabasco sauce
- 7 tsp. cumin, divided
- 3 T. pepper, divided
- 4 tsp. cayenne pepper, divided
- 6 C. flour

PREPARATION

Pour frying oil into fryer pot. Set fryer to medium-high setting and heat oil until the deep-fry thermometer reaches 350°F; it should take about 20+ minutes. Meanwhile, divide chickens into drumsticks, wings, and breast pieces. In a medium bowl, combine buttermilk, Tabasco sauce, 3½ teaspoons cumin, 1½ tablespoons pepper, and 2 teaspoons cayenne pepper, whisking until smooth. In a separate bowl, combine flour and remaining cumin, pepper, and cayenne pepper. Dip chicken pieces in buttermilk mixture and then coat in flour mixture. Shake off excess flour and roll again in flour mixture. Slowly place coated chicken pieces into the oil. Fry chicken until golden brown. Remove chicken from oil with a slotted spoon or using the fryer basket and set on paper towels to drain.

SOUTHERN FRIED CHICKEN Makes 16 servings

INGREDIENTS

- Frying oil
- 4 (3 lb.) whole chickens
- 6 T. salt, divided
- Water to cover chicken
- 2 C. flour
- 3 tsp. pepper
- 3 tsp. cayenne pepper
- 2 tsp. dried thyme

PREPARATION

Divide chickens into drumsticks, wings, and breast pieces. In a large bowl, place chicken pieces and sprinkle with 4 tablespoons salt. Cover chicken with water and refrigerate at least 2 hours. Pour frying oil into fryer pot. Set fryer to medium-high setting and heat oil until the deep-fry thermometer reaches 360°F; it should take about 25+ minutes. Meanwhile, drain chicken. In a medium bowl, combine flour, pepper, cayenne pepper, dried thyme, and remaining 2 tablespoons salt. Dip chicken pieces in flour mixture until well coated. Slowly place coated chicken pieces into the oil. Fry chicken until golden brown. Remove chicken from oil with a slotted spoon or using the fryer basket and set on paper towels to drain.

FRIED CHICKEN Makes 12 servings

INGREDIENTS
- Frying oil
- 3 whole chickens
- 3 T. Lawry's seasoned salt
- 6 cloves garlic, minced
- 3 C. flour

PREPARATION
Pour frying oil into fryer pot. Set fryer to medium-high setting and heat oil until the deep-fry thermometer reaches 375°F; it should take about 30+ minutes. Meanwhile, divide chickens into drumsticks, wings, and breast pieces. In a medium bowl, combine seasoned salt and minced garlic. In a separate bowl, place flour. Roll chicken pieces in garlic mixture and then in flour. Shake off excess flour and roll again in seasonings. Slowly place covered chicken pieces into the oil. Fry chicken until golden brown. Remove chicken from oil with a slotted spoon or using the fryer basket and set on paper towels to drain.

CORNISH HENS Makes 4 servings

INGREDIENTS

- 1 T. kosher salt
- ¼ tsp. pepper
- 1 T. onion powder
- 1½ tsp. garlic powder
- 1 tsp. cayenne pepper
- 4 Cornish hens, completely thawed
- 2 gallons peanut oil (see Note 1 on page 17)

PREPARATION

In a small bowl, combine kosher salt, pepper, onion powder, garlic powder, and cayenne pepper. Stir until seasonings are fully combined. Rub seasoning mixture to coat all surfaces of the Cornish hens. Place hens in the fryer basket or on the rack, neck side down. Add measured amount of peanut oil to the fryer pot (see Note 1 on page 17). Set fryer to medium-high setting and heat oil until the deep-fry thermometer reaches 350°F; it should take about 30+ minutes. Slowly lower hens into the oil. Fry hens for about 3 minutes per pound plus 5 minutes, using the weight of the heaviest Cornish hen. For example, if the heaviest hen weighs 2 pounds. The cooking time would be 2 x 3 + 5, for a total cooking time of 11 minutes. Carefully remove the hens from the hot oil and let drain for about 10 minutes.

DELICIOUS PRIME RIB Makes 8 to 12 servings

INGREDIENTS

- 3 to 4 gallons peanut oil (see Note 1 on page 17)
- 1 (4 to 6 lb.) boneless beef prime rib roast
- 3 C. dry red wine
- 1 C. olive oil
- 2 T. wine vinegar
- 1 tsp. garlic powder
- 2 tsp. onion powder
- 2 tsp. salt
- 3 T. Grey Poupon mustard
- 3 T. horseradish sauce
- 3 T. lime juice
- 2 T. cayenne pepper

PREPARATION

Add measured amount of peanut oil to a 7 to 10 gallon fryer pot (see Note 1 on page 17). Set fryer to medium-high setting and heat oil until the deep-fry thermometer reaches 350°F; it should take about 30+ minutes. Meanwhile, wrap prime rib roast completely with plastic wrap. In a blender, combine red wine, olive oil, wine vinegar, garlic powder, onion powder, salt, mustard, horseradish sauce, lime juice, and cayenne pepper. Process until liquefied. Using a poultry injector, inject marinade into prime rib, injecting 1½ to 2 ounces of marinade per pound of meat. Remove plastic wrap and pat prime rib with paper towels until dry. Sprinkle with additional cayenne pepper and salt. Place prime rib on frying rack or in fryer basket. Lower prime rib into oil (see Note 9 on page 17). Fry roast for 45 minutes to 1 hour (about 10 minutes per pound). When prime rib has been cooked to 160°F, carefully remove from the hot oil and turn off the fryer. Allow prime rib to drain for a few minutes on paper towels. Cover rib roast with aluminum foil and let rest for 10 minutes before carving.

PORK TENDERLOINS Makes 16 servings

INGREDIENTS

- 3 to 4 gallons peanut oil (see Note 1 on page 17)
- 4 (1 lb.) pork tenderloins
- 3 C. dry red wine
- 1 C. olive oil
- 2 T. wine vinegar
- 1 tsp. garlic powder
- 2 tsp. onion powder
- 2 tsp. salt
- 2 T. cayenne pepper

PREPARATION

Add measured amount of peanut oil to a 7 to 10 gallon fryer pot (see Note 1 on page 17). Set fryer to medium-high setting and heat oil to 350°F; it should take about 30+ minutes. Meanwhile, wrap pork tenderloins completely with plastic wrap. In a blender, combine red wine, olive oil, wine vinegar, garlic powder, onion powder, salt, and cayenne pepper. Mix well until liquefied. Using a poultry injector, inject marinade into tenderloins, using 1½ to 2 ounces of marinade per pound of meat. Remove plastic wrap and pat tenderloins with paper towels until dry. Sprinkle with additional cayenne pepper and salt. Place tenderloins on frying rack or in fryer basket. Lower tenderloins into oil (see Note 9 on page 17). Fry tenderloins for 48 minutes to 1 hour (about 12 to 15 minutes per pound). When tenderloins are cooked to 160°F, carefully remove from the hot oil and turn off the fryer. Allow tenderloins to drain for a few minutes on paper towels.

STUFFED PORK CHOPS Makes 16 servings

INGREDIENTS

- Frying oil
- 16 (8 oz.) pork chops
- 1 lb. ground Italian sausage
- 2 C. finely chopped onions
- 2 C. dry breadcrumbs
- 6 C. flour
- 2 C. cornstarch
- 2 T. garlic salt
- 4 eggs
- 3 C. milk

PREPARATION

Pour frying oil into fryer pot. Set fryer to medium-high setting and heat oil until the deep-fry thermometer reaches 350°F; it should take about 20+ minutes. Meanwhile, make 1½" slits in the side of each pork chop on the side opposite the bone, being careful not to slice all the way through the chops. In a medium bowl, combine ground sausage, chopped onions, and breadcrumbs. Stuff sausage mixture into the slits inside pork chops until all is used. Close chops with wooden toothpicks. In a large bowl, combine flour, cornstarch, and garlic salt. In a separate bowl, combine eggs and milk. Dredge stuffed chops in flour mixture and dip into egg mixture. Dredge again in flour mixture. Slowly place stuffed pork chops into the oil. Fry pork chops until golden brown. Remove pork chops from oil with a pair of long tongs and set on paper towels to drain.

DEEP-FRIED STEAK Makes 4 steaks

INGREDIENTS

- 3 to 4 gallons peanut oil (see Note 1 on page 17)
- 4 steaks of desired thickness
- 3 T. coarse salt
- 3 T. paprika
- 2 T. pepper
- 1 T. garlic powder
- 1 T. onion powder
- 1 T. dried thyme

PREPARATION

Add measured amount of peanut oil to a 7 to 10 gallon fryer pot (see Note 1 on page 17). Set fryer to medium-high setting and heat oil until the deep-fry thermometer reaches 350°F; it should take about 30+ minutes. Meanwhile, in a medium bowl, combine coarse salt, paprika, pepper, garlic powder, onion powder, and dried thyme. Rub seasoning into steaks until thoroughly coated. Place steaks on frying rack or in fryer basket. Lower steaks into oil (see Note 9 on page 17). Fry steaks according to chart below. When steaks are tender, carefully remove from the hot oil and turn off the fryer. Allow steaks to drain for a few minutes on paper towels.

Thickness	Medium Rare	Medium	Well Done
½"	1 Minute	2 Minutes	3 Minutes
¾"	2 Minutes	3 Minutes	4 Minutes
1"	3 Minutes	4 Minutes	5 Minutes
1¼"	4 Minutes	5 Minutes	6 Minutes

★★★★ MAN CAVE TIP ★★★★

DEEP-FRYING A STEAK

Blasphemy? Nope. Just like broiling and grilling, deep-frying is a method of dry-heat cooking, the appropriate technique for preparing a tender cut of beef like a rib-eye. All three methods cook hot and fast while creating a flavorful brown crust on the exterior of the meat. So, assuming you don't leave the steak in the fryer too long because you're arguing how overrated Joe Namath was, a deep-fried steak should emerge to the perfect Man Cave specs: medium-rare and juicy.

VENISON CUTLETS Makes 16 servings

INGREDIENTS

- 16 (4 oz.) venison cutlets
- 6 C. buttermilk, divided
- 4 T. plus 1 tsp. Cajun seasoning
- ¼ C. butter, melted
- Frying oil
- 3 C. flour
- 3 C. cornstarch
- 4 tsp. garlic powder
- 2 tsp. dry mustard
- 4 large eggs

PREPARATION

Place venison cutlets between waxed paper and, using a meat mallet, pound meat to ¼" thickness. In a medium bowl, combine 4 cups buttermilk, 1 teaspoon Cajun seasoning, and melted butter. Place venison cutlets in large plastic bags and pour buttermilk mixture over venison. Seal bags and refrigerate overnight. Pour frying oil into fryer pot. Set fryer to medium-high setting and heat oil until the deep-fry thermometer reaches 350°F; it should take about 20+ minutes. Meanwhile, drain venison and discard buttermilk mixture. In a large bowl, combine flour, cornstarch, remaining 4 tablespoons Cajun seasoning, garlic powder, and dry mustard. In a separate bowl, combine eggs and remaining 2 cups buttermilk. Dredge venison pieces in flour mixture, shaking off excess. Dip venison in batter, shake off excess, and dredge again in flour mixture. Slowly lower battered venison into the oil. Fry cutlets for 2 to 3 minutes. Remove cutlets from oil and set on paper towels to drain.

CALZONES Makes 32 calzones

INGREDIENTS

- Frying oil
- 1½ C. shredded mozzarella cheese
- ½ C. finely chopped Genoa salami
- ¼ C. grated Romano cheese
- 2 tsp. dried basil
- 2 egg yolks
- 2 (10 oz.) tubes refrigerated pizza dough
- Spaghetti sauce

PREPARATION

Pour frying oil into fryer pot. Set fryer to medium-high setting and heat oil until the deep-fry thermometer reaches 350°F; it should take about 20+ minutes. Meanwhile, in a medium bowl, combine mozzarella cheese, chopped salami, Romano cheese, dried basil, and egg yolks. Mix until well combined. Unroll pizza dough on a lightly floured flat surface. Roll dough into two 12" squares, evening the edges with a ruler. Cut each square into sixteen 3" squares. Place 1½ teaspoons of the cheese mixture in the center of each square. Brush the edges of the squares lightly with water and fold squares over filling to make a triangle, pressing down on edges to seal. Press down on edges with a fork to securely enclose the filling. Slowly place filled calzones into the oil. Fry calzones for 3 to 4 minutes, turning once, until golden brown. Remove calzones from oil with a slotted spoon or using the fryer basket and set on paper towels to drain. Serve with spaghetti sauce for dipping.

CAJUN CHICKEN NUGGETS Makes 12 servings

INGREDIENTS

- Frying oil
- 2 lb. boneless, skinless chicken breast halves
- 1 tsp. salt
- 1 tsp. pepper
- 2 eggs
- ⅔ C. club soda
- ⅔ C. flour
- 3 tsp. cayenne pepper
- 3 tsp. onion powder
- 2 tsp. dried thyme
- 2 tsp. garlic powder

PREPARATION

Pour frying oil into fryer pot. Set fryer to medium-high setting and heat oil until the deep-fry thermometer reaches 360°F; it should take about 25+ minutes. Meanwhile, cut chicken breast halves into 1½" squares. Season chicken squares with salt and pepper. In a medium bowl, combine eggs and club soda. Add chicken pieces, turning until coated and let stand for 15 minutes, turning once. On a large sheet of waxed paper, combine flour, cayenne pepper, onion powder, dried thyme, and garlic powder. Remove chicken pieces from egg mixture, shaking off excess and roll into seasoning on waxed paper. When all chicken pieces are coated, dip chicken pieces again into the egg mixture. Slowly place coated chicken nuggets in oil. Fry nuggets for 5 to 6 minutes. Remove nuggets from oil with a slotted spoon or using the fryer basket and set on paper towels to drain.

TURKEY FRYER HOT WINGS Makes 4 to 6 servings

INGREDIENTS

- Peanut, canola, or safflower oil
- 3 lb. chicken wings
- ½ C. melted butter
- ½ C. hot sauce

PREPARATION

Pour oil into a turkey fryer bucket and heat to 375° to 400°. Carefully lower wings, one at a time, into hot oil. Cook for 10 to 15 minutes or until cooked through and lightly browned. Remove wings from fryer bucket and drain on paper towels. Meanwhile, in a small bowl, combine melted butter and hot sauce, mixing well. Place about ⅓ of the cooked chicken wings and ⅓ of the sauce mixture into a large bowl with a lid. Place lid on bowl and shake until wings are evenly coated with sauce. Remove wings to a serving tray and repeat with remaining wings and sauce. Serve with Blue Cheese Dressing or Home-Style Ranch Dressing (page 109).

VARIATIONS

Maple-Flavored Wings: Add ¼ cup maple syrup to sauce before tossing with wings.

BBQ Wings: Simply toss cooked wings in BBQ sauce instead of butter and hot sauce.

BUFFALO WINGS Makes 24 to 36 wings

INGREDIENTS

- ➢ Frying oil
- ➢ 1 T. butter
- ➢ 2 (12 oz.) bottles Louisiana Red Hot sauce
- ➢ 1 (5 oz.) bottle Tabasco sauce
- ➢ Pinch of garlic powder
- ➢ Pinch of Worcestershire sauce
- ➢ Dash of soy sauce
- ➢ 1 T. ketchup
- ➢ 1 T. water
- ➢ 1 T. cornstarch
- ➢ 24 to 36 chicken wings

PREPARATION

Pour frying oil into fryer pot. Set fryer to medium-high setting and heat oil until the deep-fry thermometer reaches 350°F; it should take about 20+ minutes. Meanwhile, in a large saucepan over medium heat, place butter. When butter has melted, stir in Red Hot sauce, Tabasco sauce, garlic powder, Worcestershire sauce, soy sauce, and ketchup. Let mixture simmer for 15 minutes. In a small bowl, combine water and cornstarch. Blend cornstarch mixture into hot sauce mixture until thickened. Slowly place the chicken wings into the oil. Fry chicken wings until golden brown. Remove wings from oil and set on paper towels to drain. Place hot sauce mixture in a large plastic container with a tight fitting lid. Add drained chicken wings to hot sauce in the container. Close container with lid and shake until well coated.

PO' BOY SANDWICHES Makes 16 sandwiches

INGREDIENTS

- Frying oil
- 6 lb. shrimp, peeled and deveined
- 4 eggs
- 4 tsp. salt
- 2 tsp. garlic powder
- 1 tsp. dried oregano
- ½ tsp. pepper
- 2 C. flour
- 4 C. cornmeal
- 4 (16 oz.) loaves French bread, sliced in half horizontally
- Mayonnaise
- Creole mustard
- 4 C. shredded cabbage
- 2 ripe tomatoes, thinly sliced

PREPARATION

Pour frying oil into fryer pot. Set fryer to medium-high setting and heat oil until the deep-fry thermometer reaches 375°F; it should take about 30+ minutes. Meanwhile, rinse shrimp under cool water and pat dry completely. In a medium bowl, combine eggs, salt, garlic powder, dried oregano, and pepper, beating until frothy. On two separate large sheets of waxed paper, place flour and cornmeal. Dredge the shrimp in the flour and dip in the egg mixture. Roll shrimp in cornmeal and place on wire racks until all shrimp are coated. Slowly place coated shrimp into the oil. Fry each batch of shrimp for 1 to 2 minutes or until golden. Remove shrimp from oil with a slotted spoon or using the fryer basket and set on paper towels to drain. To assemble sandwiches, spread inside of French loaves with desired amount of mayonnaise and Creole mustard. Layer sandwiches with shredded cabbage, tomato slices and fried shrimp. Cut each loaf into 4 sandwiches.

★★★★ MAN CAVE HALL OF FAME ★★★★

THE SANDWICH

Did you know that the sandwich was quite possibly created in a Man Cave? Legend has it that the word *sandwich* originated in 1762 during a card game involving the English aristocrat John Montagu, the 4th Earl of Sandwich. As his night of gambling rolled on and his stomach started to growl, he ordered a waiter to bring him roast beef between two slices of bread. Too busy to stop gambling, he ordered the inaugural sandwich to keep his fingers from getting greasy while playing cards. Rumor has it the other participants began to order "...the same as Sandwich."

While the sandwich is a first-ballot Man Cave Hall of Famer, it's hard to believe there is no official Sandwich Hall of Fame.

If one opened tomorrow, here's the inaugural class of inductees:

- BLT
- Club
- Grilled Cheese
- Po'Boy
- Philly Cheesesteak
- Muffuletta
- Cubano
- Lobster Roll
- Reuben
- French Dip
- Fried Egg
- Sub
- PB&J
- Monte Cristo

FRIED CLAMS Makes 10 servings

INGREDIENTS

- ➤ Frying oil
- ➤ 8 C. shucked hard-shelled clams
- ➤ 2 eggs
- ➤ 4 tsp. seafood seasoning
- ➤ 1 C. flour
- ➤ 2 C. dry breadcrumbs

PREPARATION

Pour frying oil into fryer pot. Set fryer to medium-high setting and heat oil until the deep-fry thermometer reaches 375°F; it should take about 30+ minutes. Meanwhile, drain clams and reserve ¼ cup of the clam juice. In a medium bowl, combine eggs, seafood seasoning, and reserved ¼ cup clam juice with a fork until well mixed. Place flour and dry breadcrumbs into two separate shallow bowls. Dredge the clams in the flour and dip into the egg mixture. Roll the clams in the breadcrumbs and place on a wire rack. Slowly place coated clams in oil. Fry clams for 4 to 5 minutes. Remove clams from oil with a slotted spoon or using the fryer basket and set on paper towels to drain.

CRISPY SHRIMP Makes 30 servings

INGREDIENTS
- Frying oil
- 8 lb. large shrimp, fresh or frozen
- 4 C. flour
- 4 T. Cajun seasoning
- 6 C. Bisquick baking mix
- 8 C. club soda

PREPARATION
Pour frying oil into fryer pot. Set fryer to medium-high setting and heat oil until the deep-fry thermometer reaches 350°F; it should take about 20+ minutes. Meanwhile, thaw shrimp completely and peel, leaving the tails intact. Devein shrimp, rinse, and pat dry. In a medium bowl, combine flour and Cajun seasoning. In a separate bowl, combine baking mix and club soda. Coat shrimp in flour mixture, shaking off excess, and dip into batter mixture. Dredge shrimp again in flour. Slowly place coated shrimp in oil. Fry shrimp for 2 to 3 minutes. Remove shrimp from oil with a slotted spoon or using the fryer basket and set on paper towels to drain.

POPCORN SHRIMP Makes 16 servings

INGREDIENTS

- ➤ Frying oil
- ➤ 4 lb. small shrimp, peeled and deveined
- ➤ 4 eggs
- ➤ 4 tsp. salt
- ➤ 4 tsp. cayenne pepper
- ➤ 2 tsp. garlic powder
- ➤ 1 tsp. dried thyme
- ➤ 1 tsp. dried oregano
- ➤ ½ tsp. pepper
- ➤ 2 C. flour
- ➤ 4 C. cornmeal

PREPARATION

Pour frying oil into fryer pot. Set fryer to medium-high setting and heat oil until the deep-fry thermometer reaches 375°F; it should take about 30+ minutes. Meanwhile, rinse shrimp under cool water and pat dry completely. In a medium bowl, combine eggs, salt, cayenne pepper, garlic powder, dried thyme, dried oregano, and pepper, beating until frothy. On two separate large sheets of waxed paper, place flour and cornmeal. Dredge the shrimp in the flour and dip in the egg mixture. Roll shrimp in cornmeal and place on wire racks until all shrimp are coated. Slowly place coated shrimp into the oil. Fry each batch of shrimp for 1 to 2 minutes or until golden. Remove shrimp from oil with a slotted spoon or using the fryer basket and set on paper towels to drain.

CALAMARI Makes 24 servings

INGREDIENTS

- Frying oil
- 2 C. cornmeal
- 2 C. flour
- 4 lb. fresh or frozen squid, cut into ½" rings

PREPARATION

Pour frying oil into fryer pot. Set fryer to medium-high setting and heat oil until the deep-fry thermometer reaches 375°F; it should take about 30+ minutes. Meanwhile, in a large bowl, combine cornmeal and flour. Rinse squid pieces and pat dry thoroughly with paper towels. Add squid pieces to flour mixture and toss until fully coated. Slowly place coated squid into the oil. Fry squid for about 3 minutes, until golden brown. Remove calamari from oil with a slotted spoon or using the fryer basket and set on paper towels to drain.

★★★★ MAN CAVE TIP ★★★★

BUYING FISH

First things first: a fish market should not smell. If it smells like low tide, run in the other direction. When you find a good fish market, get to know the delivery schedule and get there when the fresh fish arrives.

When it comes to calamari and shrimp, unless they were freshly caught and delivered, buy frozen. They're fresher. Once they're caught out at sea, they're immediately frozen for shipment. If you don't buy them frozen, you have no clue how long they've been defrosted.

For fish fillets, look for shiny and metallic skin. And, again, use your beak: if they smell pungent, keep shopping. Any liquid on the fillets? Clear, good; milky, bad...very bad.

Buy your shellfish—mussels, clams, and oysters—at the best market you can find. They are sold alive so you don't want them spending too much time behind the glass; the faster they sell, the fresher they'll be. Tap them and they should close up. Very important: unless you want food poisoning, get rid of any that haven't opened after cooking. They were dead before they hit the pan.

Same goes for lobster and crabs; look for ones that are moving around the tank, blissfully unaware of their future.

CORN FRITTERS Makes 48 fritters

INGREDIENTS

- Frying oil
- 2 C. flour
- 2 tsp. baking powder
- 2 tsp. sugar
- 1½ tsp. salt
- ½ tsp. white pepper
- 4 eggs, separated
- 1 C. milk
- 4 T. butter, melted
- 3 C. fresh, frozen, or canned whole corn kernels

PREPARATION

Pour frying oil into fryer pot. Set fryer to medium-high setting and heat oil until the deep-fry thermometer reaches 375°F; it should take about 30+ minutes. Meanwhile, in a medium bowl, combine flour, baking powder, sugar, salt, and white pepper. In a small bowl, lightly beat egg yolks, milk, and melted butter. Stir butter mixture into flour mixture just until combined. Add corn kernels. In a medium mixing bowl, beat egg whites until stiff peaks form. Fold egg whites into corn mixture. Slowly drop tablespoonsful of the corn batter into the oil. Fry fritters for 3 to 4 minutes or until golden. Remove fritters from oil with a slotted spoon or using the fryer basket and set on paper towels to drain.

VEGETABLE EGG ROLLS Makes 48 rolls

INGREDIENTS

- 6 T. dark sesame oil
- 3 C. shredded carrots
- 3 C. thinly sliced shitake mushrooms
- 3 C. snow peas, thinly sliced
- 3 tsp. fresh minced garlic
- 3 tsp. fresh minced gingerroot
- 3 C. finely shredded green cabbage
- 6 green onions, thinly sliced
- ¾ C. teriyaki sauce
- Frying oil
- 3 (16 oz.) packages egg roll wrappers
- 3 large eggs, well beaten

PREPARATION

In a large skillet over medium-high heat, heat sesame oil. Add shredded carrots, sliced mushrooms, snow peas, minced garlic, and minced gingerroot. Sauté for 4 minutes and remove from heat. Let cool and add shredded cabbage, sliced green onions, and teriyaki sauce. Mix well. Pour frying oil into fryer pot. Set fryer to medium-high setting and heat oil until the deep-fry thermometer reaches 350°F; it should take about 20+ minutes. Meanwhile, spoon ⅓ cup of the filling mixture into the center of each egg roll wrapper. Fold top corner down over filling and tuck under filling. Fold left and right corners over filling. Lightly brush remaining corner with beaten egg. Tightly roll filled end toward corner and press gently to seal. Slowly place egg rolls into the oil. Fry 10 to 12 egg rolls at a time. Immediately check the oil temperature and increase the flame so the oil temperature is maintained at 350°. If the oil temperature drops to 340° or below, oil will begin to seep into the egg rolls. Fry egg rolls for 2 to 3 minutes or until golden brown, turning once. Remove egg rolls from oil and set on paper towels to drain. Serve warm.

DEEP-FRIED CAULIFLOWER, MUSHROOMS & ZUCCHINI Makes 30 servings

INGREDIENTS

- ➤ Frying oil
- ➤ 2 large heads cauliflower
- ➤ 2 (16 oz.) packages whole mushrooms
- ➤ 2 large zucchinis
- ➤ 6 C. dry breadcrumbs
- ➤ 6 large eggs
- ➤ 1 C. milk

PREPARATION

Pour frying oil into fryer pot. Set fryer to medium-high setting and heat oil until the deep-fry thermometer reaches 375°F; it should take about 30+ minutes. Meanwhile, remove outer leaves from cauliflower. Rinse cauliflower, mushrooms, and zucchinis under cool water and pat dry completely. Break cauliflower into small florets and cut zucchinis into ½"-thick slices. In a shallow bowl, place breadcrumbs. In a separate bowl, using a whisk, thoroughly combine eggs and milk. Dip cauliflower florets, mushrooms, and zucchini slices into egg mixture. Roll vegetables in breadcrumbs until fully coated. Slowly place coated vegetables into the oil. Fry each batch of vegetables for 1 to 2 minutes or until golden. Remove vegetables from oil with a slotted spoon or using the fryer basket and set on paper towels to drain.

★★★★ MAN CAVE TIP ★★★★

MULTI-TASKING

The next time you hit the road for a camping trip or homecoming tailgate, bring along your versatile turkey fryer. Not only will it deliver some delicious food, but it'll also pull double duty when packing and cleaning up. You can jam it full of those small, easy-to-lose items you need for the trip, it can double as a large pot for dishwashing, and it's got handles. Just fill it half full of water and set the fryer on low. When the water reaches the desired temperature (don't let it boil), add dish soap. Wash all your dirty dishes, then rinse the turkey fryer well to remove any soap residue from the pot.

FRIED RAVIOLI Makes 24 servings

INGREDIENTS

➤ Frying oil
➤ 2 C. flavored croutons
➤ 4 large eggs
➤ 1 C. milk
➤ 4 (9 oz.) packages refrigerated 4-cheese ravioli
➤ Marinara sauce

PREPARATION

Pour frying oil into fryer pot. Set fryer to medium-high setting and heat oil until deep-fry thermometer reads 375°F—about 30+ minutes. Process croutons in blender on high until finely ground, then place in a shallow dish. In a medium bowl, combine eggs and milk. Dip ravioli in egg mixture and roll in crushed croutons. Slowly place coated ravioli in oil and fry for 8 to 10 minutes. Remove ravioli from oil with a slotted spoon or using the fryer basket and set on paper towels to drain. Serve ravioli with marinara sauce.

DIPPING SAUCE Makes 3 cups

INGREDIENTS

➤ 2 C. chicken broth
➤ ⅔ C. soy sauce
➤ ⅔ C. dry sherry
➤ 3 tsp. sugar
➤ 2 tsp. fresh grated gingerroot
➤ 4 T. sliced green onions

PREPARATION

In a medium saucepan over low heat, combine chicken broth, soy sauce, sherry, sugar, and gingerroot. Bring to a boil, reduce heat, and let simmer for 5 minutes. Remove from heat and let cool. Stir in sliced green onions. Goes great with Vegetables Tempura.

VEGETABLES TEMPURA Makes 10 servings

INGREDIENTS

- Frying oil
- 2 sweet potatoes
- 2 red or green bell peppers
- 24 small mushrooms
- 2 large cucumbers
- 3 C. flour
- 3 tsp. baking powder
- 1 tsp. salt
- 2 egg whites
- 2½ C. ice water

PREPARATION

Pour frying oil into fryer pot. Set fryer to medium-high setting and heat oil until the deep-fry thermometer reaches 375°F. Meanwhile, cut vegetables into ¼" slices. In a large bowl, combine flour, baking powder, and salt. In a separate bowl, combine egg whites and water. Sift the flour mixture into the egg white mixture, stirring until slightly lumpy. Dip vegetables into the batter mixture, shaking off the excess. Slowly place some of the vegetables into the oil. Fry each batch of vegetables until golden brown. Remove vegetables from oil with a slotted spoon or using the fryer basket and set on paper towels to drain. Goes great with Dipping Sauce.

★★★★ MAN CAVE FILM FEST ★★★★

TOP 10 SAMURAI MOVIES

If you enjoy classic westerns depicting the "man with no name" stoically battling injustice or the wandering gunslingers defending an innocent town from the tyranny of evil, then you'll enjoy a good samurai movie with your tempura and cold beer.

- **Seven Samurai**
- **Harakiri**
- **Yojimbo**
- **Ran**
- **Sanjuro**
- **The Twilight Samurai**

- **Ghost Dog: The Way of the Warrior** Modern take with mob theme.
- **The Last Samurai**
- **13 Assassins**
- **Zatoichi**

HUSH PUPPIES Makes 30 hush puppies

INGREDIENTS
- Frying oil
- 3 C. cornmeal
- 3 C. flour
- 1 C. sugar
- 2 tsp. baking powder
- Pinch of baking soda
- Pinch of garlic salt
- Salt and pepper to taste
- 1 (15 oz.) can cream-style corn
- 2 large green peppers, diced
- 2 large onions, diced
- 2 eggs

PREPARATION
Pour frying oil into fryer pot. Set fryer to medium-high setting and heat oil until the deep-fry thermometer reaches 375°F; it should take about 30+ minutes, depending on the amount of oil, outside temperature, and wind conditions. Meanwhile, in a large bowl, combine cornmeal, flour, sugar, baking powder, baking soda, garlic salt, salt, pepper, cream style corn, diced green peppers, diced onions, and eggs. Mix until well blended. Slowly drop tablespoonfuls of the batter into the oil. Fry hush puppies for 4 to 5 minutes or until golden. Remove hush puppies from oil with a slotted spoon or using the fryer basket and set on paper towels to drain.

FRIED SPINACH BALLS Makes 18 servings

INGREDIENTS
- Frying oil
- 6 C. chopped, cooked spinach
- 6 T. butter, melted
- 6 T. minced onions
- 6 T. grated Parmesan cheese
- Salt and pepper to taste
- 6 eggs, divided
- 5 C. dry breadcrumbs, divided
- ⅜ tsp. allspice
- ¾ C. water

PREPARATION
Pour frying oil into fryer pot. Set fryer to medium-high setting and heat oil until the deep-fry thermometer reaches 360°F; it should take about 20+ minutes, depending on the amount of oil, outside temperature, and wind conditions. Meanwhile, in a large bowl, combine cooked spinach, melted butter, minced onions, Parmesan cheese, salt, pepper, 3 eggs, 3 cups breadcrumbs, and allspice. Mix well and let stand for 10 minutes. In a separate bowl, whisk together remaining 3 eggs and water. Place remaining 2 cups dry breadcrumbs in a shallow dish. Roll spinach mixture into balls. Dip balls in egg mixture and then roll in breadcrumbs. Slowly place spinach balls in oil. Fry spinach balls until golden brown. Remove spinach balls from oil with a slotted spoon or using the fryer basket and set on paper towels to drain.

FRIED DILL PICKLES Makes 24 servings

INGREDIENTS
- Frying oil
- 2 (32 oz.) jars sliced dill pickles
- 4 C. cornmeal
- 1 T. Cajun seasoning

PREPARATION
Pour frying oil into fryer pot. Set fryer to medium-high setting and heat oil until the deep-fry thermometer reaches 350°F; it should take about 20+ minutes. Meanwhile, drain pickles, rinse, and pat dry completely. In a large plastic bag, combine cornmeal and Cajun seasoning. Add drained pickles to bag. You may have to coat pickles in batches. Seal bag and shake until well coated. Slowly place coated pickles into the oil. Fry each batch of pickles for 1 to 2 minutes or until golden. Remove pickles from oil with a slotted spoon or using the fryer basket and set on paper towels to drain.

JALAPEÑO POPPERS Makes 24 servings

INGREDIENTS

➤ Frying oil
➤ 48 fresh whole jalapeno peppers
➤ 48 slices Monterey Jack or cheddar cheese, cut into 1½" strips
➤ 1 C. flour
➤ 2 T. Cajun seasoning
➤ 1½ C. buttermilk
➤ Ranch dressing, optional

PREPARATION

Pour frying oil into fryer pot. Set fryer to medium-high setting and heat oil until the deep-fry thermometer reaches 350°F; it should take about 20+ minutes. Meanwhile, cut a slice in each pepper lengthwise on one side. Remove seeds and stuff each pepper with a piece of cheese. In a medium bowl, using a whisk, combine flour and Cajun seasoning. Slowly pour buttermilk into flour mixture, stirring until smooth. Dip stuffed peppers into batter, coating on all sides. Slowly place 10 to 12 peppers into the oil. Fry each batch of peppers for 2 minutes or until golden. Remove peppers from oil with a slotted spoon or using the fryer basket and set on paper towels to drain. If desired, serve with ranch dressing.

HOMEMADE TORTILLA CHIPS Makes 32 servings

INGREDIENTS
- Frying oil
- 2 (25 oz.) packages 8" corn tortillas
- Salt or Cajun seasoning
- Salsa, optional

PREPARATION
Pour frying oil into fryer pot. Set fryer to medium-high setting and heat oil until the deep-fry thermometer reaches 350°F; it should take about 20+ minutes. Meanwhile, cut corn tortillas into quarters. Slowly place a handful of cut tortillas into the oil. Fry each batch of tortilla chips for 1 minute or until golden, turning once. Remove chips from oil and set on paper towels to drain. Sprinkle with salt or Cajun seasoning. If desired, serve warm chips with salsa.

ONION MUMS Makes 6 onion blossoms

INGREDIENTS

- Frying oil
- 3½ C. flour, divided
- 6 tsp. paprika, divided
- 2 tsp. garlic powder
- 1½ tsp. pepper, divided
- ¼ tsp. cayenne pepper
- ⅓ C. cornstarch
- 2 tsp. garlic salt
- 1 tsp. salt
- 2 (12 oz.) cans of beer
- 6 large Walla Walla sweet onions

PREPARATION

Pour frying oil into fryer pot. Set fryer to medium-high setting and heat oil until the deep-fry thermometer reaches 375°F; it should take about 30+ minutes. Meanwhile, in a medium bowl, combine 2 cups flour, 4 teaspoons paprika, garlic powder, ½ teaspoon pepper, and cayenne pepper. In a large bowl, combine remaining 1½ cups flour, cornstarch, garlic salt, remaining 2 teaspoons paprika, salt, remaining teaspoon pepper, and beer. Mix well. Cut onions into quarters from top of onion to within ½" of the base, leaving the base intact. Cut the onion in quarters again and gently spread slices apart to form petals. Cover onions in flour mixture, shaking off excess, and dip in batter. Slowly lower battered onions into the oil, petals facing up. Fry onions for 3 minutes. Remove onions from oil with a slotted spoon and let cool slightly. Carefully spread petals as far apart as possible and lower into hot oil again, petals facing down, and fry for an additional 3 minutes. Remove onions and set on paper towels to drain.

APPLE BBQ SAUCE Makes 2 gallons

INGREDIENTS
- 8 C. ketchup
- 2 T. white pepper
- 4 C. apple juice concentrate
- 2¾ C. peeled diced apples
- 2 C. apple cider vinegar
- 2 C. diced onions
- 2 C. soy sauce
- 5½ tsp. diced green peppers
- 2 T. garlic powder

PREPARATION
In the turkey fryer pot, combine ketchup, white pepper, apple juice concentrate, diced apples, apple cider vinegar, diced onions, soy sauce, diced green peppers, and garlic powder. Set fryer setting to low and bring sauce to a boil, stirring frequently with a long spoon. Reduce heat to very low and let simmer for 15 minutes, stirring frequently. If you prefer smooth sauce, carefully transfer sauce to a blender or food processor in batches and puree until smooth. Using a funnel, transfer sauce to gallon jugs. Cover jugs tightly and store sauce in refrigerator until ready to use.

RACK OF RIBS Makes 4 to 6 racks

INGREDIENTS
- 4 to 6 (2 lb.) racks of ribs
- Water
- ½ C. salt
- ¼ C. minced garlic
- 2 T. dried thyme
- ¼ C. celery salt

PREPARATION
Place racks of ribs in turkey fryer pot and fill with water to cover. Remove ribs from water and stir salt, minced garlic, dried thyme, and celery salt into the water. Return racks of ribs to seasoned water and set fryer setting to medium. Bring water to a boil. Reduce heat, cover fryer with lid, and let water simmer for 1½ hours. Remove ribs from water. Ribs are now ready for additional seasonings and to be placed over indirect heat on grill for 45 minutes. Smother ribs with your favorite BBQ sauce for last 15 minutes of grilling time.

LOBSTER BOIL Makes 2 lobsters

INGREDIENTS

- 2 whole live lobsters
- Water
- Salt
- Juice of 3 to 4 lemons

PREPARATION

Fill the fryer pot of the turkey fryer with enough water to cover both lobsters. Set fryer to medium setting and bring water to a boil. Lightly salt the water and add lemon juice. When water is fully boiling, add live lobsters, headfirst, into the water. Return water to a boil and reduce heat to low. Cover fryer pot with lid and let simmer for 5 minutes for the first pound. Cook lobsters for an additional 3 minutes per extra pound. Remove lobsters from water as soon as they are fully cooked and serve. Twist off each large claw. Remove claw meat by cracking with nutcracker. Hold the body of the cooked lobsters with a towel and twist off the tails. Remove tail meat by separating the tail shell with fingers.

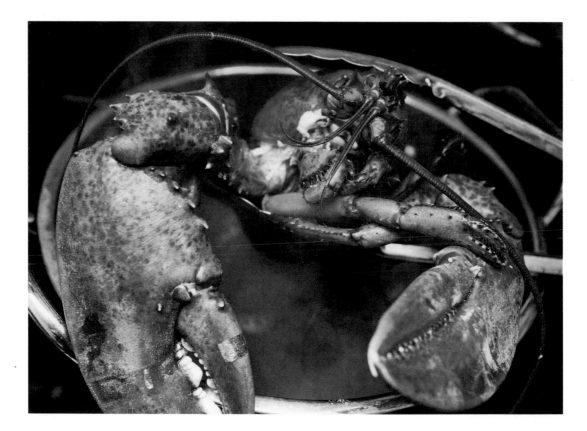

CRAB & CRAWFISH BOIL Makes 16 to 20 servings

INGREDIENTS

- Water
- 2 lb. kosher salt
- 3 lb. small red potatoes
- 6 lemons, halved
- 3 oranges, halved
- 4 heads garlic, halved
- 3 large onions, halved
- 6 packets Zatarain's Crab Boil
- 1 C. Tabasco sauce
- ½ C. red pepper flakes
- 8 large ears of corn, shucked and halved
- 3 Dungeness crabs, cracked and quartered
- 2 lb. Gulf shrimp
- 25 lb. Louisiana crawfish

PREPARATION

Fill turkey fryer pot halfway with water and salt. Set fryer to medium-high setting and bring water to a boil. It should take about 10+ minutes to heat the water. When water is boiling, add fryer basket to fryer. Place potatoes, lemons, oranges, garlic, onions, Crab Boil packets, Tabasco sauce, and red pepper flakes in fryer basket. Reduce heat and let mixture simmer for 30 minutes, covered, until potatoes are tender. Add corn and return mixture to a boil. Add crabs, shrimp, and crawfish. Cover turkey fryer and turn off the heat. Let seafood steep for about 6 minutes in hot liquid until fully cooked. Remove fryer basket from turkey fryer and let ingredients drain of water. Pour entire basket of food onto newspaper in middle of table and encourage everyone to eat from the table.

LOW COUNTRY BOIL Makes 16 servings

INGREDIENTS

- Water
- 4 bags Crab Boil mix
- 4 lb. whole new potatoes
- 16 pieces short ear corn
- 2 lb. link sausages, precooked
- 2 lb. shrimp, shelled and deveined
- 2 lb. crawfish

PREPARATION

Fill turkey fryer pot halfway with water. Set fryer to medium-high setting and bring water to a boil. It should take about 10+ minutes to heat the water. Add Crab Boil mix bags. When water is boiling, add potatoes. After potatoes have been in boiling water for 6 minutes, add corn. After 3 minutes, add precooked sausage links. After an additional 3 minutes, add shrimp and crawfish. Total cook time should be about 27 minutes. To serve, cover picnic table with thick paper or newspaper. Remove fryer basket from turkey fryer and let ingredients drain of water. Pour entire basket of food onto newspaper in middle of table and encourage everyone to eat from the table—Louisiana style!

STEAMED HALIBUT Makes 3 pounds

INGREDIENTS

- 6 green onions, chopped
- 12 fresh mushrooms, sliced
- 12 Napa cabbage leaves, sliced
- 2 T. fresh minced gingerroot
- 4 cloves garlic, minced
- 3 lb. halibut fillets, or other fish
- ½ C. soy sauce
- ¼ C. water
- Crushed red pepper flakes to taste

PREPARATION

Fill turkey fryer pot with 2" water and place fryer setting to medium heat. Bring water to a boil. Meanwhile, line the bottom of the turkey fryer basket with aluminum foil, folding up the aluminum foil to cover the sides of the basket as well. Arrange green onions, mushroom slices, cabbage slices, minced gingerroot, and minced garlic into fryer basket over aluminum foil. Place halibut fillets over vegetables in basket. Drizzle soy sauce and water over fish and vegetables. When water is boiling in fryer pot, place filled basket in fryer and cover fryer with lid. Steam fish and vegetables for 15 to 20 minutes, or until fish flakes easily with a fork.

TOP SIRLOIN CHILI Makes 32 servings

INGREDIENTS

- ½ C. vegetable oil
- 8 onions, chopped
- 12 cloves garlic, minced
- 4 lb. ground beef
- 3 lb. beef sirloin, cubed
- 4 (14½ oz.) cans diced tomatoes in juice
- 4 (12 oz.) cans dark beer

- 4 C. strong brewed coffee
- 8 (6 oz.) cans tomato paste
- 4 (14 oz.) cans beef broth
- 2 C. brown sugar
- ¾ C. chili powder
- ¼ C. cumin seeds

- ¼ C. cocoa powder
- 4 tsp. dried oregano
- 4 tsp. cayenne pepper
- 4 tsp. ground coriander
- 4 tsp. salt
- 8 (15 oz.) cans kidney beans, drained, divided
- 8 fresh hot chili peppers, seeded and chopped

PREPARATION

In the turkey fryer pot, place vegetable oil, chopped onions, minced garlic, ground beef, and cubed sirloin. Set fryer to low heat and cook for 10 minutes, stirring often with a long spoon, until ground beef and sirloin are fully browned and tender. Mix in diced tomatoes in juice, beer, coffee, tomato paste, and beef broth. Add brown sugar, chili powder, cumin seeds, cocoa powder, dried oregano, cayenne pepper, ground coriander, and salt. Stir in four cans of the drained kidney beans and chopped chili peppers. Reduce heat to very low, cover pot, and let simmer for 1½ hours, stirring frequently. Stir in remaining four cans kidney beans and simmer for an additional 30 minutes.

OMELETS IN BAGS Makes up to 60 servings

INGREDIENTS

- ➢ Water
- ➢ Small Ziplock bags, 1 per person
- ➢ Chopped onions
- ➢ Eggs, 2 per person
- ➢ Shredded cheddar cheese
- ➢ Cooked diced bacon
- ➢ Chopped green peppers
- ➢ Salt
- ➢ Pepper

PREPARATION

Fill the turkey fryer pot ¾ full with water. Set fryer to medium setting and bring water to a boil. Have each person write his or her initials on a bag with a permanent marker, crack two eggs into the bag, and add shredded cheese, bacon, onions, green peppers, salt, and pepper as desired. Seal the bags, working the ingredients together by hand. Release any air from the bags and seal again. Drop filled bags into water and cook for about 4 minutes, until eggs are fully cooked. Open bags and roll omelets out onto plates.

FRENCH TOAST Makes 16 to 20 servings

INGREDIENTS

- ➢ Frying oil
- ➢ 4 (13 oz.) loaves French bread
- ➢ 16 eggs
- ➢ 1 C. sugar
- ➢ ¼ C. milk
- ➢ ¼ C. vanilla
- ➢ Powdered sugar for dusting

PREPARATION

Pour frying oil into fryer pot. Set fryer to medium-high setting and heat oil until the deep-fry thermometer reaches 350°F; it should take about 20+ minutes. Meanwhile, cut bread into 1"-thick slices. In a large bowl, whisk together eggs, sugar, milk, and vanilla. Dip slices into the egg mixture until fully saturated. Slowly place bread slices into the oil. Fry bread slices for about 3 minutes, until golden brown. Remove French toast from oil with a pair of long tongs and set on paper towels to drain. Dust with powdered sugar before serving.

CRISPY POTATO SKINS Makes 16 servings

INGREDIENTS
- 16 large baking potatoes, scrubbed
- Frying oil
- Salt and pepper to taste
- Sour cream

PREPARATION
Before leaving for your camping trip, prick potatoes with a fork and bake in a 400° oven until tender, about 1 hour. Remove potatoes and let cool. Cut baked potatoes in half lengthwise and scoop out potato flesh. Reserve potato flesh for another use. Cut skins in half again. Set fryer to medium-high setting and heat oil until the deep-fry thermometer reaches 375°F; it should take about 30+ minutes. Sprinkle potato skins with salt and pepper. Slowly place potato skins into the oil. Fry potatoes for about 2 to 3 minutes, or until golden. Remove potatoes from oil with a slotted spoon or using the fryer basket and set on paper towels to drain. Sprinkle with additional salt and pepper to taste. Serve with sour cream for dipping.

CORN DOGS Makes 20 corn dogs

INGREDIENTS

- ➤ Frying oil
- ➤ 2 (16 oz.) packages of 10 hotdogs
- ➤ 20 (12" or longer) wooden dowels
- ➤ 1½ C. flour
- ➤ 1⅓ C. cornmeal
- ➤ ¼ C. sugar
- ➤ 3 tsp. baking powder
- ➤ ½ tsp. salt
- ➤ 1½ C. milk
- ➤ 2 eggs

PREPARATION

Pour frying oil into fryer pot. Set fryer to medium-high setting and heat oil until the deep-fry thermometer reaches 375°F; it should take about 30+ minutes. Meanwhile, pat hotdogs dry with paper towels. Insert wooden dowels into hotdogs. In a large bowl, combine flour, cornmeal, sugar, baking powder, and salt. In a separate bowl, combine milk and eggs. Add milk mixture to cornmeal mixture and stir until well blended. Dip hotdogs into batter mixture until fully coated. Slowly dip corndogs into the oil, holding onto the other end of the dowels. Be sure to wear heavy rubber gloves to avoid burns from splashing oil. Fry corndogs for about 2 to 3 minutes, until golden brown. Remove corndogs from oil and set on paper towels to drain and cool.

DEEP-FRIED BEER CHICKEN Makes 4 servings

INGREDIENTS

- ➤ 1½ C. flour
- ➤ 1 T. margarine, melted
- ➤ 1 egg, beaten
- ➤ 1 C. flat beer, room temperature
- ➤ 2 lb. chicken, cut, washed, and patted dry
- ➤ Oil for deep-frying

PREPARATION

At least 4 hours before cooking (can be done night before), mix flour, margarine, egg, and sufficient beer to make a thick paste. Spread over chicken parts; cover and refrigerate. Heat 2" to 3" of oil in deep fryer to 365°. Fry chicken pieces, a few at a time, for 15 to 20 minutes or until golden brown. Be sure to move the pieces around in the oil so they do not stick, but turn them carefully so the coating does not break off. Drain on paper towel before serving.

BEER BATTER FOR FISH Makes 3 to 4 servings

INGREDIENTS
- ½ C. baking mix
- ½ C. cornstarch
- 2 eggs, separated
- 1 T. salt
- 1 tsp. paprika
- 1 tsp. lemon pepper
- ½ C. warm beer, not light
- 3 to 4 medium-sized pieces of fish, any kind, patted dry

PREPARATION
Mix dry ingredients, egg yolks, and beer. Stir thoroughly. Whip egg whites until foamy. Fold egg whites into mixture. Coat dry fish with batter. Deep-fry at 350° until done.

★★★★ MAN CAVE TIP ★★★★

SAFETY

OK, we're just checking in to make sure you paid attention to the opening section on safety. As you are now aware, the fryer is one of the greatest culinary tools ever invented. Used properly, your turkey fryer can make anything taste good. Drop in a shoe and 3 minutes later you have the makings for a great-tasting sandwich. But the key word is *properly*. There's a reason why scalding oil was used to combat castle attacks: if it hits your skin, it hurts. A lot. Be careful when using your fryer. Wear gloves, long sleeves, and eye protection. And keep the pots of oil away from everyone—especially the kids and pets. (And, again, don't fry drunk.)

COCONUT SHRIMP Makes 6 to 8 servings

INGREDIENTS

- ➤ 1 egg
- ➤ ¾ C. all-purpose flour, divided
- ➤ ⅔ C. beer
- ➤ 1½ tsp. baking powder
- ➤ 2 C. flaked coconut
- ➤ 24 shrimp
- ➤ 3 C. oil for frying

PREPARATION

In medium bowl, combine egg, ½ cup flour, beer, and baking powder. Place ¼ cup flour and coconut in two separate bowls. Hold shrimp by tail and dredge in flour, shaking off excess flour. Dip in egg/beer batter; allow excess to drip off. Roll shrimp in coconut and place on a baking sheet lined with wax paper. Refrigerate for 30 minutes. Meanwhile, heat oil in deep fryer until the deep-fry thermometer reaches 350°. Fry shrimp in batches; cook, turning once, for 2 to 3 minutes or until golden brown. Using tongs, remove shrimp to paper towels to drain. Serve warm with your favorite dipping sauce.

BEER BATTER FOR ONION RINGS Makes 4 servings

INGREDIENTS

- ➤ ¼ C. flour
- ➤ ¼ C. cornstarch
- ➤ ¼ C. beer
- ➤ ¼ tsp. pepper
- ➤ ½ tsp. seasoning salt
- ➤ ¼ tsp. paprika
- ➤ 2 egg whites, beaten
- ➤ 3 medium onions, sliced as rings
- ➤ Oil for frying

PREPARATION

Combine first six ingredients in a small bowl. Fold beaten egg whites into batter. Dip onion rings into batter and then deep fry until golden.

BEER BATTER FRIED MOZZARELLA STICKS Makes 32 mozzarella sticks

INGREDIENTS

- Oil for frying
- 1 envelope onion soup mix
- 1 C. all-purpose flour
- 1 tsp. baking powder
- 2 eggs
- ½ C. beer
- 1 T. mustard
- 16 mozzarella sticks, unwrapped and cut in half

PREPARATION

In deep fat fryer, heat oil until the deep-fry thermometer reaches 375°. Meanwhile, in a large bowl, beat onion soup mix, flour, baking powder, eggs, beer, and mustard until smooth and well blended. Let batter stand 10 minutes. Dip cheese in batter, and then carefully drop into hot oil. Fry, turning once, until golden brown; drain on paper towels. Serve warm.

FRIED ICE CREAM Makes 16 servings

INGREDIENTS
- 2 C. finely chopped pecans
- 2 quarts vanilla ice cream, slightly softened
- 6 large eggs
- 4 C. finely crushed vanilla wafers
- Frying oil

PREPARATION
Line two baking sheets with waxed paper. Place chopped pecans in a shallow dish. Scoop vanilla ice cream into sixteen ½ cup balls, rounding with an ice cream scoop. Roll ice cream balls in pecans until fully coated. Place ice cream balls on prepared baking sheets and place in freezer overnight. Place beaten eggs in a bowl and place crushed vanilla wafers in a shallow dish. Dip each ice cream ball in the egg mixture and roll in crushed wafers until fully covered and return to freezer for 3 hours. Pour frying oil into fryer pot. Set fryer to medium-high setting and heat oil until the deep-fry thermometer reaches 375°F; it should take about 30+ minutes. Slowly place ice cream ball into the oil. Fry ice cream for 30 to 45 seconds or until outside is crispy. Remove ice cream from oil with a slotted spoon and place on serving dishes. Serve immediately.

DEEP-FRIED MARS BARS Makes 15 servings

INGREDIENTS
- Frying oil
- 15 Mars or Milky Way candy bars
- 6 C. flour
- 3 C. corn flour
- 1 T. baking soda
- 2 C. milk

PREPARATION
Chill candy bars in refrigerator until needed. Mix flours, baking soda, and milk. Heat oil until the deep-fry thermometer reaches 375°F. Coat bar thoroughly in batter and carefully lower into oil. Fry until batter is golden brown, usually about 3 to 4 minutes.

FUNNEL CAKES Makes 15 cakes

INGREDIENTS
- Frying oil
- 8 eggs, lightly beaten
- 6 C. milk
- 1 C. brown sugar
- 8 C. flour
- 2 T. baking powder
- 1 tsp. salt
- Powdered sugar
  for dusting

PREPARATION
Pour frying oil into fryer pot. Set fryer to medium-high setting and heat oil until the deep-fry thermometer reaches 375°F; it should take about 30+ minutes. Meanwhile, in a medium bowl, combine eggs, milk, and brown sugar. In a separate bowl, combine flour, baking powder, and salt. Add egg mixture to flour mixture, stirring until well combined. When oil temperature reaches 375° on a deep-fry thermometer, place 1 cup of the batter into a funnel, holding finger over the funnel spout so the batter does not drip through the funnel. Carefully hold funnel several inches above the hot oil and release finger so batter falls into hot oil. Quickly move funnel in a spiral motion until all of the batter is released. Fry funnel cake for 2 minutes on each side, flipping carefully with long tongs. Remove funnel cake from oil with long tongs and set on paper towels to drain. Repeat with remaining batter. Sift powdered sugar over funnel cakes.

APPLE FRITTERS Makes 40 fritters

INGREDIENTS

- Frying oil
- 4 C. flour
- ½ C. sugar
- 2 T. baking powder
- 1 tsp. nutmeg
- 2 tsp. salt
- 4 eggs
- 2 C. milk
- 8 large apples, peeled and cored
- Powdered sugar for dusting

PREPARATION

Pour frying oil into fryer pot. Set fryer to medium-high setting and heat oil until the deep-fry thermometer reaches 375°F; it should take about 30+ minutes. Meanwhile, in a large bowl, combine flour, sugar, baking powder, nutmeg, and salt. In a separate bowl, whisk together eggs and milk. Stir milk mixture into flour mixture until batter is smooth. Slice apples into ½" rings. Dip apple rings in batter mixture, shaking off excess. Slowly place battered apples into the oil. Fry fritters, turning once, until golden. Remove fritters from oil and set on paper towels to drain. Dust with powdered sugar before serving.

FRIED BANANAS Makes 24 servings

INGREDIENTS

- Frying oil
- 2 C. cake flour
- 2 T. sugar
- ¼ tsp. salt
- 2 eggs
- 2 C. whipping cream
- 4 C. dry breadcrumbs
- 12 ripe firm bananas
- Powdered sugar for dusting

PREPARATION

Pour frying oil into fryer pot. Set fryer to medium-high setting and heat oil until the deep-fry thermometer reaches 350°F; it should take about 20+ minutes. Meanwhile, in a large bowl, combine flour, sugar, and salt. In a separate bowl, whisk together eggs and whipping cream. Add egg mixture to flour mixture. Place breadcrumbs in a large shallow dish. Peel bananas and cut each banana in half. Dip banana halves in batter and dredge in breadcrumbs. Slowly place bananas into the oil. Fry bananas for about 3 minutes, until golden. Remove bananas from oil with a slotted spoon or using the fryer basket and set on paper towels to drain.

★ ★ ★ ★ MAN CAVE TIDBIT ★ ★ ★ ★

THE BANANA: While you're frying your bananas, consider this: they don't grow on trees; they're actually giant herbs. Really. Check it out.

CHAPTER

King of the Grill

The glory of the football gridiron may fade, but grilling greatness is a different beast altogether.

Attain it and every tailgate party, neighborhood picnic, and lazy evening in the backyard is your opportunity to perform the equivalent of that sweet touchdown dance.

To own that spot, though, you'll probably have to fight for it. All men grill, but not all men grill well. Serve up bloody chicken or burnt burgers and you'll be benched. Staying on top requires wielding mean tongs and consistently turning out the best meat + heat = crispy, juicy deliciousness they've ever eaten. Which is why you'll want this playbook—er, chapter.

AMAZING RIBS Makes 12 servings

INGREDIENTS

- ➤ 6 lb. pork baby back ribs
- ➤ Water
- ➤ 1 pinch black pepper
- ➤ 1 pinch salt
- ➤ 1 pinch crushed red pepper
- ➤ 4 C. BBQ sauce
- ➤ 2 (12 oz.) bottles porter beer, room temperature

PREPARATION

Cut ribs into small portions of 2 or 3 bones each. Bring a large pot of water to a boil. Add a pinch each of salt, black pepper, and crushed red pepper to the water. Boil ribs in seasoned water for 20 minutes. Drain off the water and let the ribs sit for about 30 minutes. Meanwhile, prepare an outdoor grill for high heat. Lightly coat the ribs with BBQ sauce. Cook the ribs over high heat for a couple of minutes on each side until they have a nice grilled look. Place grilled ribs in a slow cooker. Pour remaining BBQ sauce and one bottle of beer over the ribs; this should cover at least half of the ribs. Cook on high for 3 hours. Check ribs every 30 minutes or so and add more beer if needed to dilute sauce. If you add too much beer, the sauce will get very thin. Stir to get the ribs on top into the sauce. The ribs are done when the meat starts falling off the bone.

SEASONED PORK RIBS Makes 4 servings

INGREDIENTS
- 1 T. chili powder
- 1 T. dried parsley flakes
- 2 tsp. onion powder
- 2 tsp. garlic powder
- 2 tsp. dried oregano
- 2 tsp. paprika
- 2 tsp. pepper
- 1½ tsp. salt
- 4 lb. pork spareribs, cut into 4 racks
- BBQ Sauce (recipe on page 116)

PREPARATION
In a small bowl, combine chili powder, dried parsley flakes, onion powder, garlic powder, dried oregano, paprika, pepper, and salt. Mix well and rub over ribs. Cover ribs and let marinate in refrigerator for 2 to 8 hours. Preheat oven to 350° and place ribs in a shallow roasting pan. Bake ribs 30 minutes. Preheat grill to medium heat. Place ribs over grill and heat 10 minutes, brushing frequently with BBQ Sauce. Continue to grill until ribs are tender.

SPARERIBS Makes 6 servings

INGREDIENTS
- 4 lb. country-style spareribs, trimmed and cut in serving pieces
- 1 (12 oz.) can beer
- ½ C. dark corn syrup
- ½ C. finely chopped onions
- ⅓ C. prepared mustard
- ¼ C. corn oil
- 1 to 2 T. chili powder
- 2 cloves garlic, minced

PREPARATION
Place ribs in large shallow baking dish. In medium bowl, stir together the beer, corn syrup, onion, mustard, corn oil, chili powder, and garlic. Pour beer mixture over ribs. Cover and refrigerate overnight. Remove ribs from marinade and grill for about 40 to 45 minutes or until tender, turning and basting frequently with marinade.

LIME-MARINATED STEAK Makes 4 servings

INGREDIENTS

- ¼ C. vegetable oil
- 6 dried chili peppers, cut into strips
- 1 C. coarsely chopped onion
- 1½ tsp. minced fresh garlic
- ½ C. beef broth
- 2 T. fresh lime juice
- 2 tsp. cumin seed
- 1½ tsp. salt
- 1 tsp. brown sugar
- 4 New York steaks, tenderized
- Juice from 2 limes

PREPARATION

In a medium skillet over medium-low heat, combine vegetable oil, chili pepper strips, chopped onion, and minced garlic; sauté until onion is tender. Pour onion mixture in a blender and add beef broth, lime juice, cumin seed, salt, and brown sugar. Process until blended. Place tenderized steaks in a large sealable bag, pour half of the marinade over the steaks, and seal the bag. Place remaining marinade in an airtight container. Place bag with steaks and container with remaining marinade in refrigerator or cooler until ready to prepare. Preheat grill to medium heat. Place steaks over grill and baste with reserved marinade. Grill to taste. Before serving, brush with additional marinade and generously squeeze lime juice over cooked steaks.

BEER-MARINATED STEAKS Makes 6 servings

INGREDIENTS

- 6 (12 oz.) New York strip steaks
- 1 (12 oz.) bottle dark beer
- ½ C. brown sugar
- 6 T. lime juice
- 4 to 6 cloves garlic, chopped
- 3 T. Worcestershire sauce
- 4 T. olive oil
- 1 tsp. hot pepper sauce
- 3 T. whole grain mustard

PREPARATION

Place steaks in single layer in glass baking dish. Whisk beer, sugar, lime juice, garlic, Worcestershire, olive oil, hot pepper sauce, and mustard in large bowl to blend. Pour marinade over steaks in baking dish. Cover tightly with plastic wrap and refrigerate overnight. Remove steaks from marinade and grill to desired doneness.

GRILLED TEQUILA CHICKEN Makes 4 servings

INGREDIENTS
- 4 boneless, skinless chicken breasts
- ⅓ C. lime juice
- 2 T. jalapeño pepper jelly
- 2 T. fresh chopped cilantro
- 2 T. tequila
- 2 T. olive oil
- 1 tsp. fresh minced garlic
- ¼ tsp. salt
- ¼ tsp. pepper

PREPARATION
Rinse chicken breasts and pat dry. Arrange chicken breasts in an 8" square baking dish and set aside. In a small bowl, combine lime juice, jalapeño pepper jelly, fresh chopped cilantro, tequila, olive oil, minced garlic, salt, and pepper. Mix well and pour over chicken in baking dish. Cover baking dish and let marinate in refrigerator 2 to 8 hours. Preheat grill to medium-high heat. Place marinated chicken over grill and heat until chicken is cooked through.

BEER CAN CHICKEN Makes 4 servings

INGREDIENTS
- 1 C. butter, divided
- 2 T. garlic salt, divided
- 2 T. paprika, divided
- Salt and pepper to taste
- 1 (12 oz.) can beer
- 1 (4 lb.) whole chicken

PREPARATION
Preheat an outdoor grill for low heat and lightly oil grate. In a small skillet, melt ½ cup butter. Mix in 1 tablespoon garlic salt, 1 tablespoon paprika, and salt and pepper. Discard half the beer, leaving remainder in the can. Add remaining butter, garlic salt, paprika, and desired amount of salt and pepper to beer can. Place the beer can on a disposable baking sheet. Set the chicken on the can, so the can is in the cavity of the chicken. Baste chicken with the melted, seasoned butter. Place baking sheet with beer and chicken on the prepared grill. Cook over low heat for about 3 hours or until chicken is no longer pink and juices run clear.

★★★★ MAN CAVE TIDBIT ★★★★

WHAT KIND OF BREW FOR BEER-CAN CHICKEN?

Stouts and porters add a hint of malt; Ales and IPAs a floral note; wheat a fruity tone. American lagers add little flavor and and primarily keep the meat moist. **One opinion:** if it's in a can, it's not strong enough. Drink it and add a premium bottle of beer to the can.

CHICKEN SALAD BOATS Makes 18 servings

INGREDIENTS

- 4 packages of precooked chicken tenders (about 20 per package)
- 18 hard rolls
- 3 C. finely chopped celery
- 1 medium onion, peeled and finely chopped
- 4 T. mayonnaise
- 1 large bottle Italian salad dressing
- Salt and pepper to taste
- 18 slices provolone cheese

PREPARATION

Preheat grill to medium heat and cover the grate with aluminum foil. Grill chicken tenders until heated through, remove from grill, and cut into small pieces. Meanwhile, hollow out hard rolls by cutting a hole in the top of each roll and pulling out the bread, leaving bottom intact to make a boat shape. In a medium bowl, combine chicken tender pieces, chopped celery, chopped onion, mayonnaise, Italian salad dressing, salt, and pepper. Mix well and spoon mixture into hollowed rolls. Place rolls in a metal 9" x 13" baking dish. Place a slice of provolone cheese over each roll in baking dish. Place baking dish over heated grill until cheese melts and rolls are slightly browned. Remove from grill and serve warm.

BBQ SAUSAGE & PEPPERS Makes 6 servings

INGREDIENTS

- 2 lb. spicy Italian sausage, sliced
- 1 large red bell pepper, cut into large chunks
- ¼ lb. jalapeno peppers, cut into large pieces
- 1 large red onion, cut into chunks
- 1 (12 oz.) can beer
- ½ lb. sliced provolone cheese

PREPARATION

Place sausage, red bell pepper, jalapeno peppers, and red onion in a large bowl. Pour in beer. Cover and marinate in the refrigerator at least 1 hour. Preheat an outdoor grill for high heat and lightly oil grate. Alternately thread sausage, red pepper, jalapenos, and onion onto skewers. Cook on the prepared grill until sausage is evenly brown and vegetables are tender. Melt provolone cheese over the hot ingredients during the last few minutes of cooking.

ITALIAN SAUSAGE & PEPPERS Makes 4 servings

INGREDIENTS

- ½ C. olive oil
- ¼ C. red wine vinegar
- 2 T. fresh chopped parsley
- 1 T. dried oregano
- 2 cloves garlic, crushed
- 1 tsp. salt
- 1 tsp. pepper
- 4 hot or sweet Italian sausage links
- 1 large onion, peeled and sliced into rings
- 1 large red bell pepper, quartered

PREPARATION

In a small bowl, combine olive oil, vinegar, chopped parsley, dried oregano, crushed garlic, salt, and pepper. Place sausages, sliced onion, and quartered red bell pepper in a large sealable bag and pour marinade over ingredients in bag. Seal bag and place in refrigerator or cooler until ready to prepare. Preheat grill to medium heat. Place a heavy skillet over heated grill. Empty contents of bag into skillet and heat, covered, about 4 to 5 minutes. Continue to grill until sausages are cooked through. To serve, spoon cooked sausages and some of the onions and peppers onto each serving plate.

THE AMERICAN BURGER Makes 4 servings

INGREDIENTS

- 1½ lb. ground beef
- 2 tsp. Worcestershire sauce
- 2 T. fresh chopped parsley
- 2 tsp. onion powder
- 1 tsp. garlic powder
- 1 tsp. salt
- 1 tsp. pepper
- 4 hamburger buns, split
- Ketchup, mustard, chopped onions, relish, optional

PREPARATION

Preheat grill to medium heat. In a medium bowl, combine ground beef, Worcestershire sauce, chopped parsley, onion powder, garlic powder, salt, and pepper. Mix lightly but thoroughly. Shape mixture into four burgers, each about ½" thick. Place burgers on hot grate. Cook burgers over grill 8 to 10 minutes, turning once, until cooked as desired. Remove burgers from grate and place on buns. Garnish burgers with ketchup, mustard, chopped onions, and relish as desired.

THE CHEDDAR BURGER Makes 4 servings

INGREDIENTS
- 1 lb. ground beef
- ⅓ C. steak sauce, divided
- 4 (1 oz.) slices cheddar cheese
- 1 medium onion, peeled and cut into strips
- 1 medium green or red bell pepper, cut into strips
- 1 T. butter
- 4 hamburger buns, split
- 4 slices tomato

PREPARATION
Preheat grill to medium-high heat. In a medium bowl, combine ground beef and 3 tablespoons steak sauce. Mix lightly but thoroughly. Divide mixture into four equal parts. Shape each part into a patty, enclosing one slice of cheddar cheese inside each burger, and set aside. Place a skillet on the hot grate and cook onion and bell pepper strips in butter, heating until vegetables are tender. Stir in remaining steak sauce and keep warm. Place burgers on hot grate. Cook burgers over grill for 8 to 10 minutes, turning once, until cooked as desired. Remove burgers from grate and place on buns. Top each burger with a tomato slice and cooked onions and peppers.

BEER 'N' BRATS Makes 12 servings

INGREDIENTS
- 3 (12 oz.) cans beer
- 2¼ C. water
- 12 uncooked bratwurst
- 2 tsp. minced garlic
- 1 tsp. brown sugar
- 2 onions, peeled and sliced
- Salt and pepper to taste
- 12 brat buns
- Mustard

PREPARATION
In a medium saucepan over medium heat, combine beer, water, bratwurst, minced garlic, brown sugar, sliced onions, salt, and pepper. Mix and cook until liquid begins to boil. Reduce heat, cover, and let cook for 25 minutes, until brats are cooked through. Strain onions from cooking liquid and reserve. Place onions and brats in separate airtight containers and chill in refrigerator or in cooler until ready to prepare. Preheat grill to medium-high heat and cover a section of the grate with aluminum foil. Place onion slices on aluminum foil to warm. Place brats over grill and cook until fully browned. To serve, place one brat on each bun and top with mustard and heated onions.

BRATWURST & BEER Makes 8 servings

INGREDIENTS

- 2 lb. bratwurst
- 2 onions, thinly sliced
- 1 C. butter
- 6 (12 oz.) cans or bottles beer
- 1½ tsp. ground black pepper

PREPARATION

Prick bratwurst with fork to prevent them from exploding as they cook, then place them in a large stew pot. Add onions and butter or margarine and slowly pour beer into the pot. Place pot over medium heat and simmer for 15 to 20 minutes. Preheat grill for medium-high heat. Lightly oil grate and place bratwurst on grill. Cook for 10 to 14 minutes, turning to brown evenly. Serve hot off the grill.

CHEESE-STUFFED BRATS Makes 5 servings

INGREDIENTS

- 5 fully cooked bratwurst
- ¼ C. shredded Monterey Jack cheese
- 2 green onions, thinly sliced
- 5 strips bacon
- 5 French-style rolls or brat buns
- Ketchup, mustard, chopped onions, and relish, optional

PREPARATION

Preheat grill to medium heat. Cut a ½" wide slit lengthwise in each bratwurst. Fill the slit in each bratwurst with shredded Monterey Jack cheese, dividing cheese evenly among the bratwurst. Repeat with sliced green onions. Wrap a strip of bacon around each bratwurst to enclose the green onions and cheese. Secure bacon strips with toothpicks. Place bratwursts, cut side up, over grill and heat for 5 to 10 minutes, until bacon is crisp and cheese is melted. Place bratwursts in buns and top with ketchup, mustard, chopped onions, and relish as desired.

BUFFALO DRUMSTICKS Makes 4 servings

INGREDIENTS
- 8 large chicken drumsticks
- 3 T. hot pepper sauce
- 1 T. vegetable oil
- 1 clove garlic, minced
- ¼ C. mayonnaise
- 3 T. sour cream
- 1½ T. white wine vinegar
- ¼ tsp. sugar
- ⅓ C. crumbled blue cheese
- Celery sticks

PREPARATION
Place chicken drumsticks in a large sealable plastic bag. In a small bowl, combine hot pepper sauce, vegetable oil, and minced garlic. Pour mixture over chicken in bag. Marinate chicken in refrigerator at least 1 hour and up to 24 hours, turning occasionally. To make blue cheese dressing, combine mayonnaise, sour cream, white wine vinegar, and sugar in a small bowl. Mix well and stir in crumbled blue cheese. Store dressing and celery sticks in airtight containers until ready to serve. Preheat grill to high heat. Remove chicken from bag and discard the marinade. Place chicken on grate and grill, covered, for 25 to 30 minutes, turning three to four times. Chicken is done when it is tender and no longer pink in the middle. Serve drumsticks with blue cheese dressing and celery sticks.

SALMON SKEWERS Makes 12 servings

INGREDIENTS
- 1 lb. skinless salmon filet
- 12 wooden skewers, soaked in water
- ¼ C. soy sauce
- ¼ C. honey
- 1 T. rice vinegar
- 1 tsp. minced fresh gingerroot
- 1 clove garlic, minced
- Pinch of pepper
- 12 lemon wedges

PREPARATION
Lightly oil the grill grate and preheat grill to medium-high heat. Slice salmon filet lengthwise into 12 long strips and thread each strip on a soaked wooden skewer. Place skewers in a shallow baking dish. In a medium bowl, whisk together soy sauce, honey, vinegar, minced gingerroot, minced garlic, and pepper. Pour mixture over skewers in baking dish and let marinate at room temperature for 30 minutes. Pour remaining marinade into a small saucepan. Place saucepan over grill and bring mixture to a simmer. Thread 1 lemon wedge onto the end of each skewer. Place marinated skewers over heated grill and cook for 4 minutes on each side, brushing often with simmering marinade mixture. Salmon is done when it flakes easily with a fork.

HOT GARLIC BREAD Makes 16 servings

INGREDIENTS

- 1 C. butter
- 5½ T. minced garlic
- 2½ T. crumbled blue cheese
- 3½ T. mixed herbs
- 1 T. crushed red pepper flakes
- Sea salt and pepper to taste
- Dash of Worcestershire sauce
- 1 thin baguette, cut into thick slices

PREPARATION

Preheat grill to high heat. Place a medium saucepan over grill. Place butter in saucepan until melted and stir in minced garlic, crumbled blue cheese, mixed herbs, red pepper flakes, sea salt, pepper, and Worcestershire sauce. Mix well until thoroughly heated through. Dunk baguette slices in melted butter mixture to coat both sides. Place coated baguette slices over grill and toast for 1 minute on each side, brushing with any remaining butter mixture.

TOMATO SALAD ON THE GRILL Makes 6 to 8 servings

INGREDIENTS

- 1 T. olive oil
- 1 T. fresh lemon juice
- 2 cloves garlic, minced
- 3 dashes Worcestershire sauce
- ½ C. fresh chopped basil
- 5 large tomatoes, quartered
- Salt and pepper to taste
- ½ loaf crusty bread, torn into pieces

PREPARATION

Preheat grill to medium-high heat and cover the grate with aluminum foil. In a small bowl, whisk together olive oil, lemon juice, minced garlic, and Worcestershire sauce. Mix in chopped basil and set aside. In a medium bowl, combine quartered tomatoes, salt, and pepper. Drizzle additional olive oil over aluminum foil on grill. Turn tomatoes out onto aluminum foil on grill and heat, turning frequently, until browned. In a medium bowl, toss together grilled tomatoes and chopped basil mixture. Season with additional salt and pepper to taste. Serve tomato salad with pieces of crusty bread for dipping.

GRILLED CORN ON THE COB Makes 4 servings

INGREDIENTS

- 4 ears of corn, husks intact
- 1½ T. butter, melted
- ½ tsp. ground cumin
- ¼ tsp. chili powder
- 1 tsp. fresh chopped cilantro

PREPARATION

Preheat grill to medium heat. Pull back husks from ears of corn, leaving the husks attached. Remove one strip of husk from the inner side of each ear of corn and set aside. In a small bowl, combine melted butter, ground cumin, chili powder, and chopped cilantro. Brush melted butter mixture on corn. Bring husks up to cover corn and tie with reserved strips. Place corn on the hot grate and grill for 20 to 30 minutes, turning occasionally.

MINI ONION BLOSSOMS Makes 4 servings

INGREDIENTS

- 4 large sweet onions, peeled
- 6 T. butter, divided
- Garlic salt to taste
- Salt and pepper to taste

PREPARATION

Preheat grill to high heat. Cut each onion into quarters, keeping sections of each onion together. Place 1½ tablespoons butter and desired amount of garlic salt in the center of each onion. Wrap each onion in a double layer of aluminum foil. Place wrapped onions directly on the grill and cook for 30 to 45 minutes. Carefully remove onions from grill. Using a hot pad or oven mitt, slowly unwrap onions and season with salt and pepper.

EASY HERBED POTATOES Makes 4 to 6 servings

INGREDIENTS

- 2 T. olive oil
- 1 T. balsamic vinegar
- 1 tsp. garlic salt
- 1 tsp. dried rosemary
- ¼ tsp. pepper
- 2 small Vidalia onions, peeled and cut into wedges
- 3 large carrots, peeled and sliced diagonally
- 2 red potatoes, chopped

PREPARATION

Preheat grill to high heat or oven to 400°F. In a 9" x 13" metal baking dish, combine olive oil, vinegar, garlic salt, dried rosemary, and pepper. Add onion wedges, carrot slices, and chopped potatoes. Toss until evenly coated. Place baking dish directly over grill, cover grill, and cook, turning occasionally, until vegetables are tender, or bake for 40 minutes or until vegetables are tender.

SPICY TAILGATER'S POCKETS Makes 8 servings

INGREDIENTS

- 1 (1.25 oz.) package Caribbean-flavored marinade mix
- ¼ C. water
- 2 T. pineapple or orange juice
- 1 T. brown sugar
- 1 T. distilled white vinegar
- 1 lb. kielbasa, cut into ¼" slices
- 1 large red bell pepper, cut into strips
- 1 medium onion, peeled and sliced
- 1 pkg. pita bread or burrito-style tortillas

PREPARATION

Preheat grill to medium-high heat. In a small bowl, combine marinade mix, water, pineapple juice, brown sugar, and vinegar. Mix well and set aside. Cut aluminum foil into four 18" squares. Place an even amount of the kielbasa slices, red bell pepper strips, and onion slices in the center of each aluminum foil square. Roll aluminum foil to loosely enclose the ingredients and fold up one end, leaving one end open. Divide marinade evenly among packets and seal packets by folding down remaining open end of aluminum foil. Shake packets to coat mixture inside. Place packets on preheated grill and cook for 45 minutes, turning once. Carefully remove packets from grill and open one end. Let mixture cool for 2 to 3 minutes while letting the steam escape. To serve, divide grilled mixture into four pita bread pockets or spoon on tortillas.

VEGGIES ON THE BARBIE Makes 4 servings

INGREDIENTS

- 8 cherry tomatoes, halved
- 1½ C. corn kernels
- 1 sweet red pepper, sliced diagonally
- ½ sweet green pepper, sliced diagonally
- 1 small onion, peeled and sliced
- 1 T. fresh chopped basil
- ¼ tsp. grated lemon peel
- Salt and pepper to taste
- 1 T. plus 1 tsp. butter, cut into pieces

PREPARATION

Preheat grill to medium heat. In a large bowl, combine halved cherry tomatoes, corn, red and green pepper slices, onion slices, fresh chopped basil, grated lemon peel, salt, and pepper. Gently toss until well mixed. Cut two 12" square pieces of aluminum foil. Divide vegetable mixture in half and place each half in the center of one aluminum foil piece. Dot pieces of butter over vegetables and fold the foil to enclose vegetables in packets. Place packets on grill and cook for 15 to 20 minutes, or until vegetables are tender. Season with additional salt and pepper before serving.

PANZANELLA SKEWERS Makes 4 servings

INGREDIENTS
- 24 (1½" to 2") cubes focaccia bread
- 1 tsp. dried basil
- 1 large clove garlic, minced
- 3 T. olive oil, divided
- 16 grape or cherry tomatoes
- 16 (1") chunks red onion
- ¼ C. pesto

PREPARATION
Oil grate and preheat grill to medium heat. In a large bowl, combine bread cubes, basil, and garlic. Drizzle with 2 tablespoons of the oil; toss to coat well. Evenly thread bread cubes, tomatoes, and onions onto 8 skewers*. Brush with remaining oil. Place skewers on grate and close grill lid for 5 to 8 minutes or until bread is lightly toasted, turning occasionally. Arrange on plates and drizzle with pesto.

*If using wooden skewers, be sure to soak in water at least 30 minutes before grilling to prevent burning.

BACON-WRAPPED ONIONS Makes 6 servings

INGREDIENTS
- 3 large, sweet white onions
- 6 strips bacon
- 1 T. butter

PREPARATION
Preheat grill to medium heat. Peel onions. Using a small, sharp knife, carefully remove at 1" x 1" core from the top of each onion and discard. Place 1 tsp. butter in each onion. Wrap two strips of bacon around each onion, securing with toothpicks. Place each onion on a square of heavy-duty aluminum foil and bring the edges loosely together at the top. Grill about 45 minutes, or until onions are tender when pierced with the tip of a knife. Cool for a few minutes before removing from foil.

STUFFED GRILLED ONIONS Makes 6 onions

INGREDIENTS
- 6 large Spanish onions (about ½ lb. each)
- 2 C. dry bread cubes
- ⅔ C. chicken broth
- ¼ lb. ground Italian sausage, cooked

PREPARATION
Preheat grill to medium heat. Trim root end off each onion to make a flat bottom. Remove the top third of each onion and reserve. Hollow the centers of onions and discard, leaving two or three outer layers in place. In medium bowl, soak bread cubes in chicken broth, turning to coat. When broth is completely absorbed, add sausage. Toss gently to mix well. Fill onions with equal amounts of sausage mixture. Place tops on onions. Place each onion upright in center of a square of heavy-duty aluminum foil; bring up edges and seal, leaving a little space for steam to expand. Grill upright for 45 minutes or until very tender.

SPICY SWEET POTATOES Makes 4 servings

INGREDIENTS
- ¼ tsp. salt
- ½ tsp. ground cumin
- ½ tsp. paprika
- ¼ tsp. ground cinnamon
- ¼ tsp. chipotle powder
- 1 T. apple cider vinegar
- 2 T. olive oil
- 1½ lbs. sweet potatoes

PREPARATION
Peel sweet potatoes and slice into ½ x ½" fries. In a small bowl, mix salt, cumin, paprika, cinnamon, chipotle powder, and vinegar. Add oil slowly. Mix well and brush seasoned oil on all sides of fries. Preheat grill to medium heat and grill fries until browned on all sides, brushing frequently with oil mixture. Remove from heat and sprinkle with desired seasonings.

BLUEBERRY RHUBARB CRUMBLE Makes 6 servings

INGREDIENTS

- ➤ 3 C. fresh or frozen blueberries
- ➤ 2 C. fresh or frozen diced rhubarb
- ➤ ½ C. sugar
- ➤ ¼ C. plus 2 T. flour, divided
- ➤ ½ C. quick-cooking oats
- ➤ ½ C. brown sugar
- ➤ ¼ tsp. ground nutmeg
- ➤ ¼ tsp. ground cinnamon
- ➤ ¼ C. butter
- ➤ Whipped topping, optional

PREPARATION

In a medium saucepan over medium heat, combine blueberries, rhubarb, sugar, and 2 tablespoons of flour. Cook, stirring constantly, until bubbly and thickened. Pour mixture into an 8" square metal or foil baking pan and set aside. To make topping, in a medium bowl, combine oats, brown sugar, remaining ¼ cup flour, nutmeg, and cinnamon; mix well. Using a pastry blender, cut in butter until mixture resembles coarse crumbs. Sprinkle topping mixture over fruit mixture in baking dish. Cover pan tightly with aluminum foil. Preheat grill to medium heat. Place metal or foil pan over grill and heat for 20 to 25 minutes, or until topping is lightly browned. If desired, serve warm with whipped topping.

★★★★ MAN CAVE TIP ★★★★

THE TAILGATE CHECKLIST

While tailgates are not as complicated (or dangerous) as flying a plane, a pre-flight checklist comes in handy. Prepare one, laminate it for marking, and get packing. (And remember...the ingenuity and tricks of packing for a camping trip transfer well to tailgating.) Here are some other key tailgate tips and must-haves:

- **Fly a flag or banner on a pole**
  Friends will find you and cold beer faster.

- **Pop up some shade in the form of a canopy, umbrella, or sunscreen lotion**
  Especially for early-season SEC games.

- **Raingear**
  What applies to camping applies here.

- **Bring big garbage bags**
  Your alma mater will thank you.

- **Jumper cables**
  You'll make a friend for life.

- **Matches, charcoal, and propane**
  Tough to cook without heat.

- **Toilet paper**
  Port-a-potties ain't the Ritz; be prepared.

- **Plenty of ice and water**
  You can't have too much of either.

- **First aid kit**
  Just in case.

- **A winning attitude**
  Fly the team colors, deck out the ride, wear a jersey; heck, paint your face... but have fun and be the 12th man.

CHAPTER

3

Man of the Kitchen

Outdoors, people expect guys to cook.

Indoors, not so much—which makes the kitchen your best chance to establish a reputation as a man who really knows his way around food. Nonchalance works best. Just take an actual casserole to the next potluck where the rest of the guys contribute soda and stale chips, or whip up something for the crew to devour during the next big game. Word will get around.

Don't do it for them, though. Do it for you. Because if you cook, you can make what you like, when you like, the way you like it. Cast off the shackles of that restaurant! Untie those apron strings! Follow your stomach to food heaven!

BEER ONION SOUP Makes 6 servings

INGREDIENTS

- ¼ C. butter
- 1 lb. yellow onion, sliced finely with rings cut in half
- 2 T. flour
- ½ tsp. salt
- 1 (10½ oz.) can beef broth
- 1 (10½ oz.) can chicken broth
- 1 (12 oz.) can beer
- 6 thin slices French bread
- 6 slices mozzarella cheese

PREPARATION

Melt butter in heavy saucepan. Add onions, flour, and salt; cook for 15 minutes until golden brown. Add beef and chicken broth and beer. Cover and reduce heat; simmer for 15 to 20 minutes. Toast bread until golden brown and place one slice at the bottom of each of 6 serving dishes. Ladle soup over bread and top with cheese. Put under broiler for a few minutes to melt

BEER CHEESE SAUSAGE SOUP Makes 2 servings

INGREDIENTS

- ½ C. butter
- 1 carrot, peeled and chopped
- 1 tsp. garlic, minced
- 1 C. flour
- 2 C. chicken stock
- 2 C. milk
- 1 bay leaf
- ½ tsp. dry mustard
- 1 tsp. Worcestershire sauce
- ½ tsp. salt
- ¾ C. beer
- 3 oz. Swiss cheese, shredded
- 7 oz. cheddar cheese, shredded
- 8 oz. smoked sausage (8 links)
- Onion to taste

PREPARATION

Melt butter in saucepan. Add chopped carrot, garlic, and onion. Sauté until softened. Add flour and cook for 5 minutes, stirring often. Add remaining ingredients except for cheese and sausage. Reduce heat to low and let cook until soup has thickened, whisking often. Slowly whisk cheese into soup until combined and smooth. Cut sausage into quarters lengthwise, and then slice into ½" pieces. Sauté in separate pan until heated through. Blot excess grease and add to soup. Keep soup hot or cool and refrigerate until ready to serve.

WISCONSIN CHEESE 'N' BEER SOUP Makes 2 servings

INGREDIENTS

- 2 T. butter or margarine
- 2 T. all-purpose flour
- 1 envelope onion soup mix
- 3 C. milk
- 1 tsp. Worcestershire sauce
- 1 C. shredded cheddar cheese (4 oz.)
- ½ C. beer
- 1 tsp. mustard
- Chopped red pepper and parsley, optional

PREPARATION

In medium saucepan, melt butter and cook flour over medium heat, stirring constantly, for 3 minutes or until bubbly. Stir in onion soup mix until thoroughly blended with milk and Worcestershire sauce. Bring just to the boiling point, then simmer, stirring occasionally, for 10 minutes. Stir in remaining ingredients and simmer, stirring constantly, for 5 minutes or until cheese is melted. Garnish with additional cheese, chopped red pepper, and parsley as desired.

SPEEDY POTATO CHOWDER Makes 2 servings

INGREDIENTS

- 4 slices bacon, diced
- ½ C. chopped onion
- 1 (10¾ oz.) can condensed cream of potato soup
- ¾ C. beer
- ¾ C. water
- 1 (8 oz.) can mixed vegetables
- 1 C. sliced frankfurters
- 2 T. chopped fresh parsley

PREPARATION

In 3-quart saucepan over medium heat, cook bacon until crisp. Remove with slotted spoon and drain on paper towels. Pour off all but 1 tablespoon of bacon drippings. Cook onion in drippings, stirring occasionally, until tender. Stir in soup, beer, and water until mixed well. Add can of mixed vegetables with its liquid, meat, parsley, and reserved bacon. Heat through, stirring occasionally.

FRIED POTATOES Makes 4 servings

INGREDIENTS
- 6 slices bacon, diced
- 6 potatoes, peeled and sliced
- ½ tsp. celery seed
- ½ tsp. salt
- ¼ tsp. pepper
- 1 tsp. fresh minced parsley
- ⅛ tsp. paprika

PREPARATION
In a medium skillet over medium heat, sauté diced bacon until cooked and crispy. Let bacon drain on paper towels. Place sliced potatoes in skillet with bacon drippings. Cover skillet and fry potatoes until browned and tender, turning frequently to prevent burning. Sprinkle potatoes with celery seed, salt, pepper, minced parsley, and paprika. Add cooked bacon and stir until well mixed.

TORTILLA SALAD Makes 12 servings

INGREDIENTS
- 2 heads iceberg lettuce, torn
- 4 tomatoes, diced
- 1 large onion, peeled and chopped
- 6 C. shredded cheddar cheese
- 1 (14½ oz.) package corn tortilla chips, crushed
- 2 (12 oz.) bottles creamy ranch salad dressing
- 1 (12 oz.) jar thick and chunky salsa
- 2 lb. ground beef

PREPARATION
In a large bowl, combine torn lettuce, diced tomatoes, chopped onion, and shredded cheddar cheese. Add crushed tortilla chips and toss until evenly incorporated. Stir in ranch salad dressing and salsa. In a large skillet over medium heat, brown ground beef until cooked through. Drain off fat. Before serving, add cooked ground beef to salad and toss until well incorporated. Store in an airtight container and refrigerate or chill in cooler until ready to serve.

DELICIOUS BAKED BEANS Makes 8 servings

INGREDIENTS

- ➤ 1 lb. ground beef
- ➤ ½ C. chopped onion
- ➤ 1 lb. bacon, cut into pieces
- ➤ 1 C. ketchup
- ➤ 3 T. distilled vinegar
- ➤ 1 C. brown sugar
- ➤ 1 (16 oz.) can kidney beans, drained
- ➤ 2 (16 oz.) cans baked beans or pork and beans

PREPARATION

Preheat oven to 350°. In a large ovenproof skillet over medium heat, brown ground beef and chopped onions until cooked through; drain off fat. In a separate large skillet over medium heat, sauté bacon pieces until cooked and crispy. Remove bacon from skillet and let drain on paper towels. Add cooked, drained bacon to skillet with ground beef and onion. Mix well and stir in ketchup, vinegar, brown sugar, drained kidney beans, and baked beans. Cover skillet and bake mixture for 1½ to 2 hours.

DRUNKEN DOGS Makes 8 servings

INGREDIENTS

- 2 (16 oz.) packages beef frankfurters, cut into bite-size pieces
- 1 C. light brown sugar
- 1 (12 oz.) can or bottle beer

PREPARATION

In a medium saucepan, place the frankfurters, brown sugar, and beer. Bring to boil. Reduce heat and simmer for at least 1 hour.

BUBBLIN' BEER DOGS Makes 6 hot dogs

INGREDIENTS

- 6 deli-style beef hot dogs (1 lb. total)
- 1 (12 oz.) can beer
- 6 hot dog buns, split

PREPARATION

In a large saucepan, bring the beer to a boil over high heat. Prick each hot dog several times with a fork; add to the boiling beer and boil for 5 to 6 minutes until heated through. Serve in the buns and top with your favorite hot dog toppings.

POT ROAST IN BEER Makes 6 to 8 servings

INGREDIENTS

- ➤ 2 T. vegetable oil
- ➤ 2 lb. top round steak, trimmed
- ➤ 1 onion, chopped
- ➤ 2 stalks celery, chopped
- ➤ 1 clove garlic, minced
- ➤ 1 (10¾ oz.) can condensed cream of mushroom soup
- ➤ 1 (12 oz.) can or bottle beer
- ➤ 2 bay leaves
- ➤ 2 whole cloves

PREPARATION

Heat a roasting pan over high heat and coat bottom with oil. Sear meat on all sides. Remove from pan and set aside. Reduce heat to low and sauté onion, celery, and garlic, scraping up browned bits. Cover and cook on low for 15 minutes. Mix in cream of mushroom soup and beer. Wrap bay leaves and cloves in cheesecloth, tie with string, and add to pan. Place roast on top of vegetables, spooning some sauce over meat. Cover with foil and place lid over foil to seal well. Reduce heat and simmer for 1½ hours. Remove meat from pan and slice, then return it to the pan and spoon sauce over it. Cook an additional 30 minutes.

LAMB CHOPS BRAISED IN BEER Makes 6 chops

INGREDIENTS

- ➤ 6 (1½") lamb chops, fat trimmed off
- ➤ Salt and pepper
- ➤ 3 to 4 T. flour
- ➤ 3 T. oil
- ➤ 3 large onions, sliced
- ➤ 6 potatoes, sliced
- ➤ 1 tsp. thyme
- ➤ 1 can beer (enough to show itself under the onions and potatoes)

PREPARATION

Salt and pepper lamb chops and coat with flour. Heat the oil and trimmed fat in a skillet with a lid and sauté the chops swiftly on both sides, 2 minutes for each side. Cover the lamb chops with alternating layers of onions and potatoes, each salted and peppered with a bit of thyme. Add the beer, cover, and simmer for about 30 minutes over medium heat.

SAUSAGE WITH PEPPERS, ONIONS & BEER Makes 4 to 6 servings

INGREDIENTS

- ➤ 1½ T. olive oil
- ➤ 1½ lb. Italian sausage links
- ➤ 1 (12 oz.) can beer
- ➤ 1 red bell pepper, sliced
- ➤ 1 green bell pepper, sliced
- ➤ 1 large red onion, sliced
- ➤ 1 clove garlic, chopped
- ➤ ¼ C. plus 2 T. tomato paste
- ➤ 1 tsp. dried oregano
- ➤ 1 tsp. dried cilantro
- ➤ 1 T. hot sauce
- ➤ Salt and pepper to taste

PREPARATION

Heat olive oil in a large, heavy skillet over medium-high heat. Cook sausage until browned on all sides. Remove sausage from pan and set aside. Pour ½ can of beer and scrape sides and bottom of pan. Place the red peppers, green peppers, onions, and garlic in the pan. Stir in the remaining beer and tomato paste. Season with oregano, cilantro, hot sauce, salt, and pepper. Cover and simmer until onions and peppers are tender. Slice the sausages into bite-sized pieces and add to the peppers. Cover and simmer until the sausage is cooked through.

★★★★ MAN CAVE HALL OF FAME ★★★★

BALLPARK HOT DOGS

First made public at the Polo Grounds back in the early 1900s, the hot dog (along with its cousin, the sausage) remains one of the best reasons to go to the ballpark. Paired with a cold beer, there's nothing finer. Here are some of the best:

DODGER DOG, Dodger Stadium
Steamed or grilled, a foot long.

NATHAN'S FAMOUS, Yankee Stadium
Two words: Nathan's…Famous.

**THE CHEESE CONEY,
Great American Ballpark**
Covered with Cincy's famous Skyline Chili.

BREWER BRATWURST, Miller Field
Only stadium in the league where sausages outsell hot dogs.

SHACK-CAGO DOG, Citi Field
What happens when you let a restaurateur like Danny Meyer create a hot dog.

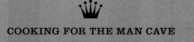

BBQ PORK CHOPS Makes 6 chops

INGREDIENTS
- ➤ 6 pork chops
- ➤ 2 T. steak seasoning
- ➤ 1 (12 oz.) can or bottle beer
- ➤ 1 (18 oz.) bottle BBQ sauce
- ➤ 2 onions, sliced

PREPARATION
Sprinkle pork chops with steak seasoning. Brown both sides in skillet. After the pork chops have been browned, remove them from the pan. Pour beer into skillet. Stir until all particles in the pan have been incorporated. Pour in BBQ sauce and place the pork chops back into the pan. Add onions and cover. Simmer on low for 1 to 2 hours.

ARROZ CON POLLO Makes 4 servings

INGREDIENTS
- ➤ 1 T. olive oil
- ➤ 1 whole chicken (2 to 3 lb.), cut into pieces
- ➤ 2 onions, chopped
- ➤ 3 cloves garlic, crushed
- ➤ ½ green bell pepper, chopped
- ➤ ½ (15 oz.) can tomato sauce
- ➤ 1 pinch saffron
- ➤ Salt to taste
- ➤ 2 cubes chicken bouillon
- ➤ 1½ C. uncooked white rice
- ➤ 1 C. beer
- ➤ 1 (15 oz.) can peas, drained
- ➤ ½ red bell pepper, roasted and sliced

PREPARATION
Heat oil in a large skillet over medium-high heat. Sauté chicken until lightly browned; remove from skillet and set aside. Sauté onion, garlic, and green bell pepper until soft; stir in tomato sauce, saffron, salt, and bouillon and return chicken pieces to skillet. Cook for 10 minutes, then add rice and reduce heat to low. Add beer and simmer for 8 to 10 minutes, stirring occasionally, until rice is tender. Finally, stir in peas with liquid and garnish with roasted bell pepper.

MARINATED VENISON Makes 6 to 8 servings

INGREDIENTS
- 2 lb. venison (deer meat)
- ½ (10 oz.) bottle Worcestershire sauce
- 1 (12 oz.) can or bottle beer
- 1½ C. all-purpose flour
- 1 T. onion salt
- 1 T. garlic powder
- Vegetable oil for frying

PREPARATION
Pound venison flat and cut into 1" strips; place in a large bowl. Pour in Worcestershire sauce and beer. Cover and refrigerate for 1 hour or more. In a shallow bowl, combine flour, onion salt, and garlic powder. Drag soaked meat through the flour mixture. Heat oil in a large, heavy skillet and fry meat until golden brown.

TIPSY CARROTS Makes 4 servings

INGREDIENTS
- 1 lb. baby carrots
- 1 T. butter
- 1 C. beer
- ¼ tsp. salt
- 1 tsp. brown sugar

PREPARATION
Rinse and cut baby carrots into quarters. In skillet, melt butter; add beer and carrots. Cook over low heat until tender, stirring often. Stir in salt and sugar. Cook for an additional 2 to 3 minutes. Serve hot.

EASY BEER & KETCHUP MEATBALLS Makes 6 servings

INGREDIENTS
- 1 (28 oz.) bottle ketchup
- 24 oz. beer
- 1½ lb. ground beef
- 2 tsp. garlic powder
- 1 onion, chopped

PREPARATION
Preheat oven to 400°. Place the beer and ketchup in a slow cooker on high setting and allow to simmer. Meanwhile, in a large bowl, combine the ground beef, garlic powder, and onion, mixing well. Form mixture into meatballs about ¾" in diameter. Place meatballs in a 9" x 13" baking dish. Bake at 400° for 20 minutes. Transfer meatballs to the slow cooker with the beer and ketchup and simmer for 3 hours; sauce will thicken.

CROCK-POT SHRIMP IN BEER Makes 3 to 4 servings

INGREDIENTS
- 2 to 3 lb. shrimp in shells
- 2 C. beer
- 2 tsp. salt
- 1 T. mixed pickling spice

PREPARATION
Wash shrimp in cold water; drain. Place in crockpot. Add remaining ingredients; stir well. Cover and cook on high setting for 2 hours or until shrimp turns pink. If desired, turn to low setting until serving time, up to 2 hours.

★★★★ MAN CAVE TIDBIT ★★★★

THE SLOW COOKER

Your new best friend. Brown meat, add vegetables and some liquid (preferably beer), and—voila!—you've got some serious comfort food. No fuss, minimal cleanup, and it can travel to a tailgate or your neighbor's man cave. Get one.

CROCK-POT BEEF IN BEER Makes 6 servings

INGREDIENTS

- 2 lb. round steak, 1" thick
- ¼ C. flour
- 1 tsp. sugar
- ⅛ tsp. pepper
- 6 to 8 small new potatoes, peeled
- 1½ oz. envelope dry onion soup mix
- ¾ C. beer

PREPARATION

Trim round steak and cut into serving portions. Combine flour, sugar, and pepper; toss with steak to coat thoroughly. Place potatoes in crockpot and cover with steak pieces. Thoroughly combine onion soup mix and beer. Pour over steak, moistening well. Cover and cook on low setting for 8 to 12 hours. Thicken gravy before serving, if desired.

★★★★ MAN CAVE TRAVEL ★★★★

TOP 10 SPORTS VENUES

No need to travel with your crock pot to these venues. This is a tough one; had to keep the list to U.S. stadiums because once you threw in the cathedrals of soccer (Wembley Stadium, anyone?) the list gets very Euro, very fast.

LAMBEAU FIELD
Green Bay Packers

FENWAY PARK
Boston Red Sox

CAMERON INDOOR STADIUM
Duke Blue Devils

COWBOY STADIUM
Dallas Cowboys

TIGER STADIUM (DEATH VALLEY)
LSU Tigers

BANKERS LIFE (CONSECO) FIELDHOUSE
Indiana Pacers

AT&T PARK
San Francisco Giants

YANKEE STADIUM
New York Yankees

SOLDIER FIELD
Chicago Bears

BEEF BRISKET IN BEER Makes 8 servings

INGREDIENTS

- 4 lb. beef brisket
- ½ tsp. pepper
- 1 large onion, sliced and separated into rings
- ½ C. chili sauce
- 3 T. brown sugar
- 2 cloves garlic, pressed
- ¾ C. light beer
- 3 T. all-purpose flour
- Pepper

PREPARATION

Trim fat from brisket and cut brisket in half. Sprinkle with ½ teaspoon pepper. Place onion rings in bottom of a slow cooker; top with brisket. Stir together chili sauce and next three ingredients; pour over brisket. Cover and cook on high for 4 to 6 hours or on low for 8 to 12 hours. Remove brisket and set aside, reserving liquid in slow cooker. Remove 1 cup reserved liquid from slow cooker; whisk in flour and pour into slow cooker, whisking constantly. Whisking constantly, cook for 5 minutes or until thickened. Serve over brisket; sprinkle with pepper.

SLOW COOKER KIELBASA & BEER Makes 6 to 8 servings

INGREDIENTS

- 2 lb. kielbasa sausage, cut into 1" pieces
- 1 (12 oz.) can or bottle beer
- 1 (20 oz.) can sauerkraut, drained

PREPARATION

In a slow cooker, combine sausage, beer, and sauerkraut. Cook on low for 5 to 6 hours until the meat is tender and plump.

EASY SLOW COOKER FRENCH DIP
Makes 6 servings

INGREDIENTS
- 4 lb. rump roast
- 1 (10½) oz. can beef broth
- 1 (10½ oz.) can condensed French onion soup
- 1 (12 oz.) can or bottle beer
- 6 French rolls
- 2 T. butter

PREPARATION
Trim excess fat from the rump roast and place in a slow cooker. Add the beef broth, onion soup, and beer. Cook on low setting for 7 hours. Preheat oven to 350°. Split French rolls and spread with butter. Bake 10 minutes or until heated through. Slice the meat on the diagonal and place on the rolls. Serve the sauce for dipping.

BEER-BATTERED CHICKEN WINGS Makes 4 servings

INGREDIENTS

- 1½ C. flour, divided
- ½ tsp. salt
- 1 C. beer
- Peanut, canola, or safflower oil
- 1½ tsp. dried parsley
- 2 T. chopped green onion
- 12 chicken wings or drumsticks
- Additional salt and pepper to taste

PREPARATION

In a medium bowl, stir together 1 cup flour and salt. Add beer, stirring until well combined. Let stand for 30 minutes. Add about 2" of oil to a large saucepan. Heat oil over medium heat to about 375°. Meanwhile, add dried parsley and chopped green onion to beer batter; stir to combine and set aside. Season chicken wings or drumsticks with salt and pepper. Place remaining ½ cup flour in a bag or bowl with a lid. Add chicken, close container, and shake to coat. Remove chicken and dip each piece in beer batter. Carefully lower wings, one at a time, into hot oil. Cook for 10 or 15 minutes or until cooked through and lightly browned. Using a long-handled metal slotted spoon, remove wings from oil and drain on paper towels.

OVEN BBQ RIBS Makes 4 servings

INGREDIENTS

- 1 (12 oz.) can or bottle beer
- 1½ C. water
- 1 T. salt
- 3 T. vegetable oil
- 5 lb. pork spareribs
- 1 T. butter
- 1 C. thinly sliced onions
- 2 cloves garlic, pressed
- 2 (8 oz.) cans diced tomatoes with juice
- 1 C. ketchup
- 3 T. molasses
- 1 T. Worcestershire sauce
- 1 T. prepared mustard
- ¼ tsp. salt
- ½ T. hot pepper sauce
- 1 T. white vinegar
- ½ lemon, sliced into rounds

PREPARATION

Pour beer and water into a large stock pot. Add salt and stir to dissolve. Bring mixture to a boil over medium-high heat. In a large skillet or frying pan, heat vegetable oil over high heat. Sear ribs on both sides. Place on paper towels to briefly drain. Add seared ribs to the beer/water mixture. Add more water as needed to cover the ribs. Cover pot and simmer for 2 hours. While the ribs are simmering, melt the butter in a saucepan and sauté the onions and garlic until onions are translucent. Stir in tomatoes, ketchup, molasses, Worcestershire, mustard, salt, hot pepper sauce, and vinegar. Bring to a slow boil, stirring constantly. Reduce heat to low and leave it simmering until the ribs are finished. Preheat oven to 350°. Drain ribs and arrange them in a shallow roasting pan or pans. Ladle the sauce over the ribs evenly, slice each lemon round in half, and distribute the half slices on top of the sauce. Cover with foil loosely and place in the oven for 15 minutes, and then uncover for the last 10, a total of 25 minutes oven time. Remove rind from lemon slices, discard rind, and return lemon "meat" to sauce on top of the ribs. Serve ribs, covering with sauce on the plate.

PRIME RIB ROAST Makes 6 servings

INGREDIENTS
- 3 tsp. grated fresh ginger root
- ⅓ C. orange marmalade
- 4 cloves garlic, minced
- 3 T. soy sauce
- 2 T. brown sugar
- ¼ tsp. hot pepper sauce
- 1 T. mustard powder
- 1 C. beer
- 1 (8 lb.) prime rib roast
- ¼ C. olive oil
- Freshly ground black pepper

PREPARATION
Mix together the ginger, marmalade, garlic, soy sauce, brown sugar, hot sauce, and mustard. Stir in the beer. Prick holes all over the roast with a two-pronged fork. Pour marinade over roast. Cover and refrigerate for at least 2 hours, basting at least twice. Preheat oven to 400°. Place roast on a rack in a roasting pan. Pour about 1 cup of marinade into the roasting pan and discard remaining marinade. Pour olive oil over roast and season with freshly ground black pepper. Insert a roasting thermometer into the middle of the roast, making sure that the thermometer does not touch any bone. Cover roasting pan with aluminum foil and seal edges tightly around pan. Cook roast for 1 hour. After the first hour, remove the aluminum foil. Baste, reduce heat to 325°, and continue roasting for 1 more hour. The thermometer reading should be at least 140° for medium-rare and 170° for well done. Remove roasting pan from oven, place aluminum foil over roast, and let rest for about 30 minutes before slicing.

CORNED BEEF Makes 12 servings

INGREDIENTS
- 4 lb. corned beef brisket
- 1 C. brown sugar
- 1 (12 oz.) can or bottle Irish stout beer

PREPARATION
Preheat oven to 300°. Rinse the beef completely and pat dry. Place the brisket on rack in a roasting pan or Dutch oven. Rub the brown sugar on the corned beef to coat entire beef, including the bottom. Pour the bottle of stout beer around and gently over the beef to wet the sugar. Cover and place in preheated oven. Bake for 2½ hours. Allow to rest 5 minutes before slicing.

OVERNIGHT PORK ROAST WITH CABBAGE Makes 8 to 10 servings

INGREDIENTS

- ➤ 4 tsp. caraway seeds, crushed and divided
- ➤ 2 cloves garlic, minced
- ➤ 2 tsp. salt
- ➤ 1 tsp. ground black pepper
- ➤ 3 lb. double loin center cut pork roast
- ➤ 3 T. olive oil, divided
- ➤ 1 onion, thinly sliced
- ➤ 4 carrots
- ➤ 2 bay leaves
- ➤ 2½ lb. fresh cabbage, shredded
- ➤ 1 (12 oz.) can or bottle beer
- ➤ 2 T. molasses
- ➤ 1 C. beef broth
- ➤ 4 potatoes, cooked and mashed
- ➤ Salt and pepper to taste

PREPARATION

In a small bowl, combine 2 teaspoons of the crushed caraway seeds, garlic salt, and ground black pepper. Rub the pork with the dry rub mixture. Cover and refrigerate for 24 hours. Preheat oven to 350°. Heat 1 tablespoon of the oil in a large skillet over medium-high heat. Add the onion, carrots, bay leaves, 1 teaspoon of the crushed caraway seeds, and salt and pepper to taste. Sauté for 8 minutes or until vegetables are tender. Transfer this to a 10" x 15" roasting pan. In the same skillet over high heat, combine ½ tablespoon of the olive oil, half (1¼ pounds) of the cabbage, and ½ teaspoon crushed caraway seeds. Sauté, stirring often, until this cooks down, about 5 to 10 minutes. Transfer this to the roasting pan and repeat with another ½ tablespoon of oil, the remaining half (1¼ pounds) of the cabbage, and the remaining crushed caraway seeds. When this has cooked down, transfer it to the roasting pan. Heat the remaining olive oil in the same skillet over medium-high heat. Place the pork loin in the heated oil and brown well on all sides. Set the roast on top of all the vegetables in the roasting pan. Add the beer and molasses to the skillet and bring to a boil, scraping up all the browned bits on the bottom of the skillet. Pour this and the broth over the pork roast and vegetables. Season with salt and pepper to taste. Bake at 350° for 45 minutes. Turn pork over and bake until the internal temperature of the pork reaches 150°. At this point, remove the pan from the oven and let the pork sit on a cutting board for 5 minutes. Slice the pork into serving-size pieces. Discard the bay leaves. Return the pork slices to the pan on top of the vegetables. Top off with the mashed potatoes. Bake at 350° for 10 to 15 minutes or until potatoes are lightly browned.

BEER SHRIMP Makes 6 to 8 servings

INGREDIENTS

- 2 lb. large shrimp, peeled and deveined with tails attached
- 1 C. beer
- 2 T. fresh parsley, chopped
- 2 T. vegetable oil
- 4 tsp. Worcestershire sauce
- 1 clove garlic, minced
- ⅛ tsp. salt
- ¼ tsp. ground black pepper
- ⅛ tsp. hot sauce

PREPARATION

Combine all ingredients in a large bowl, stirring well to coat the shrimp. Place in a large shallow dish and refrigerate. Let marinate for 2 to 3 hours, stirring occasionally. Heat oven broiler. Drain shrimp. Thread shrimp through neck and tail onto six 14" skewers so that shrimp will lie flat. Place skewers on a lightly greased rack of a broiler pan. Broil 5" from heat for 3 minutes. Turn skewers and broil for an additional 1 to 2 minutes or until shrimp turn pink. Serve warm with cold beer.

BAKED SHRIMP Makes 4 servings

INGREDIENTS

- 1 C. self-rising flour
- ¼ tsp. salt
- ¼ tsp. cayenne pepper
- ¾ C. light beer
- 1 lb. medium-sized shrimp, peeled, with tails left on, deveined and rinsed

PREPARATION

Preheat oven to 375°. Combine the flour, salt, and cayenne pepper in a medium-sized bowl. Pour the beer into the flour mixture and whisk until combined. Holding the shrimp by the tail, dip them into the batter, completely coating each shrimp. Place the shrimp about 4" apart on rimmed baking sheets that have been coated with nonstick vegetable spray. The batter will puddle around each shrimp. Bake for 12 to 14 minutes or until the coating is golden and bread-like.

BEER-BATTERED FISH Makes 12 to 14 servings

INGREDIENTS

- ¾ C. beer
- 2 eggs, separated
- ¾ C. flour
- ¾ tsp. salt
- 1½ tsp. vegetable oil
- ¼ tsp. garlic powder
- Shortening
- 25 to 30 pan fish

PREPARATION

Let beer stand at room temperature until it goes flat (approximately 45 minutes). Beat egg whites until stiff. In a separate bowl, beat the beer, flour, salt, garlic powder, oil, and egg yolks together until smooth. Fold in egg whites. Dip each fillet in the batter separately and then fry in melted shortening until brown, about 5 to 7 minutes. Turn and brown other side.

BBQ SHREDDED BEEF Makes 8 to 10 servings

INGREDIENTS

- ➤ 3 lb. beef roast
- ➤ 2 onions, chopped
- ➤ 6 tsp. Worcestershire sauce
- ➤ 2 tsp. liquid smoke flavoring
- ➤ 2 tsp. garlic powder
- ➤ 2 tsp. ground black pepper
- ➤ Salt to taste
- ➤ 2 (12 oz.) cans or bottles beer
- ➤ 2 C. water
- ➤ 1 (18 oz.) bottle BBQ sauce

PREPARATION

Preheat oven to 275°. Place roast in a large roasting pan and scatter chopped onion over it. In a large bowl, combine Worcestershire sauce, liquid smoke, garlic powder, salt, and pepper. Pour in beer, stir, and add to roasting pan. Add water to the top of beef. Cover and cook in oven at 275° for 4 to 5 hours. Shred meat with two forks. Add BBQ sauce and mix well.

BELGIUM BEEF STEW Makes 6 to 8 servings

INGREDIENTS

- 2 lb. beef stew meat, cut into 1" cubes
- ⅜ C. all-purpose flour
- ¼ C. butter
- 4 onions, diced
- 1⅔ C. water

- 1 T. white wine vinegar
- 1 sprig fresh thyme
- 2 bay leaves
- Salt and ground black pepper to taste

- 1 (12 oz.) can or bottle brown beer
- 1 slice bread
- 1 T. prepared mustard
- 2 carrots, cut into 1" pieces

- 2 T. brown sugar or more to taste

PREPARATION

Dredge the meat in the flour. In a Dutch oven, melt the butter over medium heat. Brown meat in butter, then add the onions and fry until glazed. Stir in water and vinegar. Season with thyme, bay leaves, salt, and pepper to taste. Cover and simmer for 30 minutes. Mix in the beer. Spread mustard over bread, and then add the carrots to the meat. Cover and simmer for 30 minutes. Mix in the brown sugar.

BEER STEW & DUMPLINGS Makes 12 to 14 servings

INGREDIENTS
- 4 lb. stew meat
- ½ C. flour
- ½ C. cooking oil
- 2 lb. onions, thinly sliced
- 6 cloves garlic, minced
- 3 T. brown sugar
- ¼ C. red wine vinegar
- ½ C. chopped parsley
- 2 small bay leaves
- 2 tsp. powdered thyme
- 1 tsp. salt
- Black pepper to taste
- 2 (10½ oz.) cans beef consommé
- 2 (12 oz.) cans beer
- 1 package dumpling mix, or use your own dumpling recipe

PREPARATION
Dredge meat in flour, a few pieces at a time. Brown evenly in large skillet in hot oil. As each batch is done, remove meat to large casserole (5-quart or larger). Add onion and garlic to oil in pan and cook, stirring until onions are limp and transparent. Add more oil if needed. Pour onions on top of meat. Add next seven ingredients to skillet and stir in enough beef broth to make sauce. Cook, scraping up all browned bits from bottom and sides of skillet. Pour over onions and meat. Pour remaining beef broth and 2 cans of beer on top. Cover and cook at 350° for 2 hours. Prepare dumpling batter (or your own) according to directions. Remove casserole from oven to medium heat on top of stove. Drop batter by spoonsful into hot stew. Cover; simmer for 15 minutes.

BEEF STEW Makes 6 servings

INGREDIENTS
- 1½ lb. stewing beef, cut in chunks
- Flour, for dredging
- Oil, for browning
- 1 envelope beefy onion or onion soup mix
- ½ tsp. caraway seeds
- 1 to 2 C. water
- 1 (12 oz.) can beer
- 4 carrots, cut in 2" pieces
- 4 medium potatoes, quartered
- 1 package frozen green beans or 1 small package frozen peas

PREPARATION
Dredge beef cubes in flour; brown in a couple of tablespoons of hot oil. Drain and discard any oil. Combine soup mix and caraway seeds in 1 cup water. Add to beer and then the beef cubes. Cook over low heat for at least 45 minutes until beef is almost tender. Add carrots; cook 10 minutes more. Add potatoes and green beans and cook for an additional 10 minutes until vegetables are tender. If you use green peas instead of beans, add the peas in the last few minutes. If needed, add some water to keep it from burning. Thicken with some water and cornstarch to make a nice gravy.

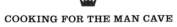

BROCCOLI CHEDDAR SOUP Makes 2 to 3 servings

INGREDIENTS

- 3 T. butter or margarine
- 1 small onion, finely chopped
- ¾ tsp. seasoning salt
- ½ tsp. garlic powder with parsley
- 6 T. all-purpose flour
- 2 C. milk
- 1½ C. chicken broth
- 1 C. beer
- 1 (10 oz.) package frozen chopped broccoli, thawed and drained
- 2½ C. (10 oz.) grated mild cheddar cheese

PREPARATION

In Dutch oven, melt butter and sauté onion, seasoning salt, and garlic powder with parsley until onion is tender. Stir in flour. Gradually whisk in milk. Bring to a boil. Reduce heat; simmer 5 minutes or until thickened. Stir in chicken broth and beer. Return to a boil. Add broccoli; reduce heat and add cheddar cheese. Stir until cheese is melted.

BEEF BEER BALLS Makes 4 servings

INGREDIENTS

- 1 lb. ground beef
- ¼ to 1 tsp. ground cloves, depending on taste
- ½ tsp. salt
- ¼ tsp. black pepper
- ½ tsp. Accent seasoning
- ½ C. ketchup
- 2 T. Worcestershire sauce
- 1 (12 oz.) can beer

PREPARATION

Mix ground beef, ground cloves, salt, pepper, and Accent. Form into small balls, about the size of walnuts. Brown well. Mix ketchup, Worcestershire sauce, and beer in separate pan; simmer for 10 minutes. Drain fat from meatballs; add sauce. Cover and simmer 2 hours. Serve on toothpicks.

BEER CHILI Makes 10 servings

INGREDIENTS

- 1 lb. chuck beef, cubed
- 1½ lbs. ground beef
- 1 lb. pork, cut into ¼" cubes
- 1 large onion
- 1 (12 oz.) can beer
- Chili powder, to taste
- 1 tsp. salt
- 1 T. oregano
- 1 (16 oz.) can kidney beans
- 1 (16 oz.) can butter beans
- 1 (16 oz.) can garbanzo beans
- 1 (#2½) can tomatoes
- 1 (15 oz.) can tomato sauce
- 1 (6 oz.) can tomato paste
- 1 (16 oz.) can mushrooms, optional
- 1 (16 oz.) can northern beans
- 1 C. beef broth, made from bouillon
- Garlic powder, to taste
- Tomato juice, as needed

PREPARATION

Brown beef, pork and onion; place in large kettle. Add all remaining ingredients. If too thick, add water and tomato juice. Simmer for several hours until flavors are blended and meat is tender.

TOMATO CURRY CHICKEN Makes 4 servings

INGREDIENTS

- 4 skinless, boneless chicken breast halves
- 2 T. butter
- 1 onion, chopped
- ⅔ C. beer
- 10¾ oz. can condensed tomato soup
- 1 tsp. curry powder
- ½ tsp. dried basil
- ½ tsp. ground black pepper
- ¼ C. grated Parmesan cheese

PREPARATION

Preheat oven to 350°. Place chicken in a 9" x 13" baking dish. Melt butter in a medium skillet over medium heat. Sauté onion, then stir in beer, soup, curry powder, basil, and pepper. Reduce heat to low and simmer for about 10 minutes, then pour over chicken. Bake at 350° for 1 hour; sprinkle with cheese for last 10 minutes of baking.

BEEF, GREEN CHILI & TOMATO STEW Makes 10 servings

INGREDIENTS

- ¼ C. vegetable oil
- 3 lb. beef chuck roast, cut into ¾" cubes
- 2 onions, chopped
- 2 cloves garlic, minced
- 1 (28 oz.) can Roma tomatoes, with juice
- 2 (4 oz.) cans chopped green chile peppers, drained
- 1 (12 oz.) can or bottle beer
- 1 C. beef broth
- 2 tsp. dried oregano, crushed
- 1½ tsp. ground cumin
- 2 T. Worcestershire sauce
- Salt to taste
- Ground black pepper to taste

PREPARATION

In a Dutch oven, heat oil over medium heat until hot, but not smoking. Pat the meat dry with paper towels and brown in batches, transferring the meat with a slotted spoon to a bowl as they are done. In the fat remaining in the pot, cook the onions until softened, about 5 minutes. Stir in the garlic and cook for 1 more minute. Return meat to the pot with any juices in the bowl and add the tomatoes with the juice, chiles, beer, beef broth, oregano, cumin, and Worcestershire sauce. Season with salt and pepper to taste. Bring to a boil and reduce heat. Simmer, partially covered for 2½ hours or until meat is tender.

DRUNKEN PINTO BEAN SOUP Makes 8 servings

INGREDIENTS

- 3 to 4 C. dried pinto beans
- 2 qts. water
- 2 to 3 slices bacon, chopped
- 1 medium onion, chopped
- 3 jalapeno peppers, seeded and chopped
- Salt, to taste
- 2 (12 oz.) cans beer

PREPARATION

Soak beans in water to cover in saucepan overnight; drain and rinse. Combine beans with 2 quarts water, bacon, and onion in saucepan. Cook over medium-low heat for several hours or until partially tender. Add peppers and salt to taste. Stir in the beer. Simmer until beans are tender and soup no longer has aroma of beer, stirring occasionally.

PORK SPRING ROLLS Makes 12 servings

INGREDIENTS

- ½ lb. ground pork
- 1 C. finely shredded cabbage
- ¼ C. finely shredded carrots
- 2 thinly sliced green onions
- 2 T. fresh chopped cilantro
- ½ tsp. sesame oil
- 1½ T. oyster sauce
- 2 tsp. fresh grated gingerroot
- 1½ tsp. minced garlic
- 1 tsp. chili sauce
- 1 T. cornstarch
- 1 T. water
- 12 (7" square) spring roll wrappers
- 4 tsp. vegetable oil

PREPARATION

Preheat oven to 425°. In a medium saucepan over medium-high heat, cook ground pork until evenly browned and cooked through. Remove from heat and drain off fat. In a medium bowl, combine cooked pork, shredded cabbage, shredded carrots, sliced green onions, fresh chopped cilantro, sesame oil, oyster sauce, grated gingerroot, minced garlic, and chili sauce. Mix until well combined. In a small bowl, combine cornstarch and water. Place about 1 tablespoon of the pork mixture in the center of each spring roll wrapper. Roll wrappers around mixture, folding edges in to enclose filling. Moisten edges of spring roll wrapper with cornstarch mixture to seal. Place filled spring rolls in a single layer on an ungreased baking sheet. Brush with vegetable oil and bake for 20 minutes, until lightly browned. For crispy spring rolls, turn rolls after 10 minutes of baking time.

BEER-CHEESE BREAD WITH ONIONS Makes 1 loaf

INGREDIENTS

➤ 3 C. flour
➤ 1 T. baking powder
➤ 1½ tsp. salt
➤ 3 T. sugar
➤ 1 C. cheddar cheese, grated
➤ 4 green onions, finely chopped
➤ 1 can beer

PREPARATION

Combine flour, baking powder, salt, sugar, cheese, and onions. Mix in beer. Pour in greased and floured loaf pan. Bake at 350° for 1½ hours.

ITALIAN PEPPERONI BEER BREAD Makes 2 loaves

INGREDIENTS

➤ 6 to 6½ C. flour, divided
➤ 2 T. dry yeast
➤ 1 C. warm water
➤ 1 C. amber lager
➤ 2 T. vegetable oil
➤ 1 T. sugar
➤ 1 T. salt
➤ ¼ C. Parmesan, Romano, or other hard cheese, grated
➤ 2 T. dried minced onion
➤ 2 T. oregano
➤ 2 tsp. rosemary, crushed
➤ 1½ tsp. black pepper, crushed
➤ 1⅓ C. finely chopped hard pepperoni
➤ 1 egg white, for brushing the loaves
➤ Cornmeal

PREPARATION

Whisk 1 cup flour and dry yeast in a large bowl. Add warm water and beer, whisk thoroughly. Cover and allow to rest in a warm place 10 to 20 minutes. Whisk in all ingredients up to the pepperoni. Stir in remaining flour one cup at a time, using your hands once dough becomes too heavy for a spatula. Continue adding flour until dough begins to pull away from the sides of the bowl. Knead vigorously by pushing, folding, and turning, adding only enough flour to prevent the dough from sticking to your hands or kneading surface. Pat dough into a flat circle and sprinkle with half of the pepperoni. Fold over and seal. Continue kneading for an additional 4 to 5 minutes. When dough becomes smooth and elastic, add the rest of pepperoni pieces until evenly distributed. Place in a lightly oiled bowl and turn over, coating the entire surface with oil. Cover and allow to rise again until doubled. Punch down and let rest for 5 minutes, covered. Form dough into the desired shape and place in lightly greased pan sprinkled with cornmeal. Allow to rise again until doubled. Brush tops with beaten egg white. Score with 4 to 5 diagonal cuts. Place bread in 350° oven and bake for 20 to 25 minutes or until loaves are golden and crusty.

DRUNK BISCUITS Makes 12 biscuits

INGREDIENTS
- 3½ C. biscuit mix
- ¼ tsp. salt
- 1 tsp. sugar
- 1½ C. beer

PREPARATION
Combine all ingredients and spoon into 12 greased muffin cups. Bake at 400° for 15 to 20 minutes until golden.

BEER & CHEESE MUFFINS Makes 12 muffins

INGREDIENTS
- 3 C. flour
- 5 tsp. baking powder
- ½ tsp. salt
- 1 T. sugar
- 1 (12 oz.) can beer
- 4 T. butter, melted
- 1 C. shredded cheddar cheese

PREPARATION
Combine flour, baking powder, salt, and sugar in bowl. Pour in beer, stirring to blend. Fill greased muffin pans ¾ full. Brush with melted butter and sprinkle with cheese. Bake at 375° for 15 to 20 minutes until browned.

THICK CRUST PIZZA Makes 1 pizza crust

INGREDIENTS
- 2 C. white flour
- 1 C. whole wheat flour
- 1 T. baking powder
- 12 oz. beer
- Pizza toppings

PREPARATION
Combine ingredients in a large bowl and mix well. Spread onto a greased 9" x 13" baking pan. Sprinkle with your favorite sauce, toppings, and grated mozzarella or other cheese. Bake at 425° for 25 to 30 minutes or until pizza is golden brown. Let stand about 10 minutes before cutting and serving.

CRISPY BAKED ONION RINGS Makes 4 to 6 servings

INGREDIENTS
- 3 egg whites
- 2 large sweet onions, peeled and cut into ¼" slices
- 2 C. finely ground cornflake crumbs
- ¼ C. flour
- 2 tsp. chicken bouillon
- 1 tsp. chili powder

PREPARATION
Preheat oven to 375°. Lightly grease a baking sheet and set aside. In a large bowl, beat egg whites at medium-high speed until foamy. Separate onion slices into individual rings. Place onion rings in bowl with egg whites and toss until evenly coated. In a separate large bowl, combine cornflake crumbs, flour, chicken bouillon, and chili powder. Mix well. Remove the coated rings from egg whites and roll several times in the crumb mixture until onion rings have desired amount of coating. Place onion rings on prepared baking sheet. Bake for 15 minutes, turning once, until coating is crispy and onions have softened.

GERMAN POTATO SALAD Makes 8 servings

INGREDIENTS

- 7 to 8 potatoes, boiled, peeled, sliced, and cooled
- 1½ C. chopped onion
- ¾ C. diced bacon
- ¾ C. vinegar
- ¾ C. flour
- 1 (12 oz.) can beer
- ¾ C. sugar
- 2 T. salt
- ¾ C. water

PREPARATION

Sprinkle cold potatoes with chopped onions; cover and let stand in refrigerator overnight, if possible. In a large skillet, fry bacon to a golden brown; add vinegar and heat to boiling. Blend flour and beer in separate bowl to make a paste; add to boiling mixture. Add sugar, salt, and water to mixture and boil for approximately 5 minutes longer. Pour hot dressing over potatoes and onions, mixing well. Let stand in warm oven (200° or less) for about 2 to 3 hours to allow flavors to blend.

DIFFERENT POTATO SALAD Makes 10 servings

INGREDIENTS

- ¾ C. mayonnaise
- ¾ C. sour cream
- ¼ C. beer
- 6 C. cooked potatoes, peeled and cubed
- ½ C. chopped onion
- ¾ C. chopped celery
- ½ lb. bacon, fried and crumbled
- Salt and pepper to taste

PREPARATION

Blend mayonnaise, sour cream, and beer together. Toss beer mixture lightly with potatoes, onion, celery, and bacon. Add salt and pepper to taste. Chill for 3 hours and serve cold or heat at 275° for 20 minutes and serve hot.

DILL POTATO SALAD Makes 4 to 6 servings

INGREDIENTS

- 4 C. diced potatoes
- 1 C. chopped celery
- 3 sliced green onions
- 3 T. vinegar
- 3 T. vegetable oil
- ¼ tsp. salt
- ¼ tsp. pepper
- ½ tsp. dried dill weed
- ¾ C. sour cream
- 2 chopped dill pickles
- 1 tomato, cut into wedges

PREPARATION

Place diced potatoes in a large pot of lightly salted water over medium heat. Bring to a boil and cook until potatoes are tender but still firm, about 15 minutes. Drain potatoes and let cool. In a large bowl, combine cooked potatoes, chopped celery, and sliced green onions. In a small bowl, combine vinegar, vegetable oil, salt, pepper, and dried dill weed. Mix well and pour over ingredients in large bowl. Toss gently until evenly coated. Chill in refrigerator overnight. Before serving, stir in sour cream and chopped dill pickles. Garnish with tomato wedges. Store in an airtight container and refrigerate or chill in cooler until ready to serve.

VEGGIE PICNIC PASTA Makes 12 servings

INGREDIENTS

- ➤ 1 lb. uncooked shell pasta
- ➤ 1 C. chopped fresh mushrooms
- ➤ 1 C. chopped cucumber
- ➤ 1 C. chopped broccoli
- ➤ 1 C. sugar
- ➤ ¾ C. vegetable oil
- ➤ ¼ C. prepared mustard
- ➤ 2 T. mayonnaise
- ➤ ¼ C. distilled white vinegar
- ➤ ¼ C. shredded cheddar cheese
- ➤ Salt and pepper to taste

PREPARATION

In a medium pot of lightly salted boiling water, cook pasta until done, about 8 to 10 minutes; drain. Rinse pasta under cool running water and let drain again. In a large bowl, combine chopped mushrooms, chopped cucumber, chopped broccoli, sugar, vegetable oil, mustard, mayonnaise, vinegar, shredded cheddar cheese, salt, and pepper. Mix well and add cooked pasta. Toss until evenly incorporated. Chill in refrigerator for 2 to 4 hours. Store in an airtight container and refrigerate or chill in cooler until ready to serve.

ITALIAN PASTA SALAD Makes 16 servings

INGREDIENTS

- ➤ 1 (16 oz.) package uncooked spiral pasta
- ➤ 3 C. halved cherry tomatoes
- ➤ ½ lb. cubed provolone cheese
- ➤ ½ lb. cubed salami
- ➤ ¼ lb. sliced pepperoni, cut in half
- ➤ 1 large green bell pepper, cut into 1" pieces
- ➤ 1 (10 oz.) can sliced black olives, drained
- ➤ 1 (4 oz.) jar pimentos, drained
- ➤ 1 (8 oz.) bottle Italian salad dressing

PREPARATION

In a medium pot of lightly salted boiling water, cook pasta until done, about 8 to 10 minutes; drain. Rinse pasta under cool running water and let drain again. In a large bowl, combine pasta, cherry tomatoes, provolone cheese, salami, and pepperoni. Add green bell pepper pieces, olives, and pimentos; toss until evenly incorporated. Pour Italian salad dressing over ingredients in bowl and toss until evenly coated. Store in an airtight container and refrigerate or chill in cooler until ready to serve.

GAME DAY PASTA SALAD Makes 4 to 6 servings

INGREDIENTS

- ➤ 1 (8 oz.) package uncooked rotini pasta
- ➤ 1 (8 oz.) package shredded Monterey Jack cheese
- ➤ ½ C. shredded carrots
- ➤ 1 (4 oz.) can sliced black olives, drained
- ➤ 1 (8 oz.) bottle Italian salad dressing
- ➤ Grated Parmesan cheese to taste
- ➤ Italian seasoning to taste

PREPARATION

In a medium pot of lightly salted boiling water, cook pasta for 8 to 10 minutes, until done; drain. Rinse pasta under cool, running water and let drain again. In a large salad bowl, combine pasta, Monterey Jack cheese, carrots, and black olives. Toss until evenly incorporated and season with Italian salad dressing, Parmesan cheese, and Italian seasoning. Store in an airtight container and refrigerate or chill in cooler until ready to serve.

★★★★ MAN CAVE DEBATE ★★★★

TOP 10 BUCKET LIST SPORTING EVENTS

There are things to do before you kick the bucket and there are things to do. As Andy said in *Shawshank Redemption*, "Get busy living, or get busy dying." Start planning that first— or next—trip.

- ■ THE MASTERS
- ■ THE FINAL FOUR
- ■ WIMBLEDON
- ■ THE SUPER BOWL
- ■ GAME 7—STANLEY CUP FINALS (especially if it's being played in Montreal)

- ■ COLLEGE BASEBALL WORLD SERIES
- ■ INDIANAPOLIS 500
- ■ KENTUCKY DERBY
- ■ TOUR DE FRANCE
- ■ WORLD CUP FINAL

SIMPLE CUCUMBER SALAD Makes 10 servings

INGREDIENTS

- 3 or 4 cucumbers, peeled and cut in ¼" slices
- 1 tsp. salt
- 1 sweet onion, peeled, cut in thin slices, and separated into rings
- 1 C. sour cream
- 2 T. sugar
- 1½ T. distilled white vinegar

PREPARATION

Place cucumber slices in a large bowl and sprinkle with salt. Place onions in bowl with cucumber. In a medium bowl, combine sour cream, sugar, and vinegar. Pour mixture over cucumbers and onions in bowl and toss until evenly coated. Store in an airtight container and refrigerate or chill in cooler until ready to serve.

B.L.T. SALAD Makes 6 servings

INGREDIENTS

- 1 lb. bacon, cut into pieces
- 8 C. shredded iceberg or romaine lettuce
- 2 large tomatoes, chopped
- 2 C. seasoned croutons
- ¾ C. mayonnaise
- ¼ C. milk
- 1 tsp. garlic powder
- ¼ tsp. salt
- ¼ tsp. pepper

PREPARATION

In a medium skillet over medium heat, sauté bacon pieces until cooked and crispy. Let bacon drain on paper towels. Place shredded lettuce in a large salad bowl. Top with a layer of chopped tomatoes, then a layer of cooked bacon. Sprinkle seasoned croutons over bacon layer. In a blender, combine mayonnaise, milk, garlic powder, salt, and pepper at medium-high speed until thoroughly blended. Before serving, pour dressing mixture over ingredients in bowl, but do not toss.

APPLE CABBAGE COLE SLAW Makes 4 servings

INGREDIENTS
- ⅓ C. plain yogurt
- 2 T. pineapple or apple juice
- ¼ tsp. mustard
- ⅛ tsp. celery seed
- 3 C. shredded cabbage
- 2 C. diced Red Delicious or Winesap apples
- 1 C. sliced celery
- ½ C. thinly sliced onion

PREPARATION
In a large bowl, whisk together yogurt, juice, mustard, and celery seed. Add shredded cabbage, diced apples, sliced celery, and sliced onion. Toss gently until completely combined. Store in an airtight container and refrigerate or chill in cooler until ready to serve.

★★★★ MAN CAVE TIDBIT ★★★★

SINGLE-MALT SCOTCH WHISKY

Things are winding down: the game was a blowout, but the meal was delicious; the cards have been dealt and you lost your shirt. It's time to bring out the single-malt and let the evening idle to a peaceful conclusion. A few things to remember:

- Make sure it's served in a snifter or a similar style glass.

- No ice. It's best slightly warm; serve it at room temperature and your hands holding the glass will do the rest.

- Serve it with a side of mineral water (sans bubbles) so a few drops can be added if necessary after an initial sniff and taste.

- Don't overdo it; with an ABV of 40%, you'll be crusty in the AM.

- Take your time. Drink it like a fine wine, not a cold beer after mowing the lawn.

BLUE CHEESE DRESSING Makes 2 cups

INGREDIENTS
- 1 C. mayonnaise
- 2 T. minced onion
- 1 T. minced garlic
- ¼ C. fresh chopped parsley
- ½ C. sour cream
- 1 T. lemon juice
- 1 T. distilled white vinegar
- ¼ C. crumbled blue cheese
- Salt and pepper to taste

PREPARATION
In a small bowl, combine mayonnaise, minced onions, minced garlic, chopped parsley, sour cream, lemon juice, vinegar, and blue cheese. Mix well and season with salt and pepper. Cover with plastic wrap and refrigerate or chill in cooler until ready to serve.

HOME-STYLE RANCH DRESSING Makes 2 ¼ cups

INGREDIENTS
- 1 C. buttermilk
- 1¼ C. mayonnaise
- 1 (1 oz.) envelope ranch dressing mix

PREPARATION
In a small bowl, combine buttermilk, mayonnaise, and ranch dressing mix. Mix until well blended. Cover with plastic wrap and refrigerate or chill in cooler until ready to serve.

EASY GARLIC SALSA Makes 1 ½ cups

INGREDIENTS

- ➤ 1 (14.5 oz.) can diced tomatoes, drained
- ➤ ½ C. olive oil
- ➤ 1 T. minced garlic
- ➤ 1 T. fresh chopped parsley
- ➤ Salt and pepper to taste
- ➤ Tortilla chips for dipping

PREPARATION

In a medium bowl, combine drained tomatoes, olive oil, minced garlic, chopped parsley, salt, and pepper. Mix until well incorporated. Cover with plastic wrap and refrigerate or chill in cooler until ready to serve. Serve with tortilla chips.

GUACAMOLE Makes 2 ½ cups

INGREDIENTS

- ➤ 3 avocados, peeled and pitted
- ➤ 1 small onion, peeled and finely chopped
- ➤ 4 cloves garlic, minced
- ➤ 1 medium tomato, chopped
- ➤ 3 T. lemon juice
- ➤ 1 small jalapeño pepper, chopped
- ➤ Salt and pepper to taste
- ➤ Tortilla chips for dipping

PREPARATION

Place peeled and pitted avocados in a large bowl. Using a fork, mash avocados until thick and slightly lumpy. Add chopped onion, minced garlic, chopped tomato, lemon juice, and chopped jalapeño pepper. Mix well and season with salt and pepper. Cover with plastic wrap and refrigerate or chill in cooler until ready to serve. Serve with tortilla chips.

ARTICHOKE DIP Makes 4 cups

INGREDIENTS

- ½ C. mayonnaise
- 2 (8 oz.) packages cream cheese, softened
- 1 (14 oz.) can artichoke hearts, drained and chopped
- 1 (10 oz.) package frozen chopped spinach, thawed and drained
- 1 C. grated Parmesan cheese
- 3 cloves garlic, minced
- 2 T. lemon juice
- Bread cubes, crackers, or tortilla chips for dipping

PREPARATION

Preheat oven to 375°. Lightly grease a 9" x 13" baking dish and set aside. In a medium bowl, combine mayonnaise and cream cheese, mixing until blended and creamy. Add artichoke hearts, spinach, and Parmesan cheese. Mix well and stir in garlic and lemon juice. Spread mixture evenly in prepared baking dish. Cover and bake for 20 minutes. Remove cover for final 5 minutes of baking time. Serve with bread cubes, crackers, or tortilla chips.

SPINACH DIP IN A BREAD BOWL Makes 3 cups of dip

INGREDIENTS

- 1 (10 oz.) package frozen chopped spinach, thawed and drained
- 1 C. sour cream
- 1 C. mayonnaise
- ¾ C. chopped green onions
- 2 tsp. dried parsley flakes
- 1 tsp. lemon juice
- ½ tsp. seasoning salt
- 1 (16 oz.) round loaf Hawaiian sweet bread

PREPARATION

In a large bowl, combine drained spinach, sour cream, mayonnaise, chopped green onions, dried parsley flakes, lemon juice, and seasoning salt. Mix until well blended and chill in refrigerator for at least 1 hour. Cut a round hole in the top of the bread loaf and remove bread from inside the loaf, leaving outer shell intact. Tear the removed bread into pieces for dipping. Spoon chilled spinach dip into hollow bread bowl and place on a serving platter. Place torn pieces of bread around bread bowl on platter. Eat the bread bowl as well!

CHEDDAR BACON STUFFED MUSHROOMS Makes 8 servings

INGREDIENTS

- ➢ 3 strips bacon
- ➢ 8 large crimini mushrooms
- ➢ 1 T. butter
- ➢ 1 T. chopped onion
- ➢ ¾ C. shredded cheddar cheese, divided

PREPARATION

Preheat oven to 400°. In a large skillet over medium-high heat, cook bacon strips until evenly browned. Remove bacon from skillet and drain on paper towels. Finely dice drained bacon. Remove stems from mushrooms, chop stems, and set caps aside. Melt butter in a large saucepan over medium heat. Add chopped mushroom stems and chopped onion. Sauté until softened. Remove from heat and place vegetable mixture in a medium bowl. Add bacon and ½ cup cheddar cheese. Mix well and spoon mixture into mushroom caps. Place filled mushroom caps in a single layer on an ungreased baking sheet. Bake for 15 minutes, until cheese has melted. Remove mushrooms from oven and sprinkle with remaining cheddar cheese.

BEER CHEESE SPREAD WITH A KICK Makes 2 cups

INGREDIENTS

- ➢ 1 (8 oz.) package shredded cheddar cheese
- ➢ 4 oz. cream cheese, softened
- ➢ ⅓ C. beer
- ➢ 1 tsp. Worcestershire sauce
- ➢ 1 tsp. chili powder
- ➢ ½ tsp. ground mustard
- ➢ ¼ tsp. cayenne pepper
- ➢ 1 tsp. dried parsley flakes
- ➢ Crackers

PREPARATION

In a blender or food processor, combine cheddar cheese, cream cheese, beer, Worcestershire sauce, chili powder, ground mustard, and cayenne pepper. Process until well incorporated and smooth. Add dried parsley flakes and mix just until blended. Remove from blender and place in a serving bowl. Cover with plastic wrap and refrigerate or chill in cooler until ready to serve. Serve with crackers.

HERBED CHEESE SPREAD Makes 2 cups

INGREDIENTS

- 1 (8 oz.) package cream cheese, softened
- 2 cloves garlic, minced
- 3 green onions, chopped
- ½ tsp. prepared mustard
- ½ tsp. Worcestershire sauce
- ¼ C. fresh chopped parsley
- ¼ C. fresh chopped dill weed
- ¼ C. fresh chopped basil
- ¼ C. chopped black olives
- 2 T. lemon juice
- Crackers or fresh vegetables

PREPARATION

In a medium bowl, combine cream cheese, garlic, green onions, mustard, Worcestershire sauce, parsley, dill weed, basil, black olives, and lemon juice, mixing until well blended. Place in a serving bowl, cover with plastic wrap, and refrigerate or chill in cooler until ready to serve. Serve with crackers or sliced vegetables.

★★★★ MAN CAVE FILM FEST ★★★★

TOP 10 POKER MOVIES

What could be more suspenseful than a guy going all in when he's down to his last ducats and the mob's breathing down his neck? How about when he extracts revenge, or orchestrates the perfect crime, while calmly playing a hand with his unsuspecting adversary? Poker movies are underrated.

- **Rounders**
- **Cincinnati Kid**
- **Maverick**
- **California Split**
- **Lock, Stock and Two Smoking Barrels**
- **Big Hand for a Little Lady** Henry Fonda gambling?
- **The Sting**
- **Ocean's Eleven** Not much poker, but too much Vegas to leave it off the list.
- **The Cooler**
- **The Gambler** The one with James Caan, not you-know-who.
- **High Roller: The Stu Unger Story** We know, this makes eleven, but we wanted to include this.

BEST CHEDDAR CHEESE DIP Makes 1 cup

INGREDIENTS

➤ 2 T. butter or margarine
➤ 1 T. flour
➤ ½ C. beer or
  non-alcoholic beer
  (not dark)
➤ 1 tsp. dry mustard
➤ 8 oz. fancy mild or sharp
  cheddar cheese, shredded

PREPARATION

Melt butter in medium saucepan over medium heat. Add flour;
cook and stir 1 minute. Add beer and mustard; heat to a boil,
stirring frequently. Stir in cheese; reduce heat to low. Stir until
cheese is melted and smooth. Transfer to small slow cooker.
Serve with breadsticks or vegetables.

CHEESY BEER & SPINACH DIP Makes 3 cups

INGREDIENTS

- ⅔ C. beer
- 3 C. shredded Monterey Jack cheese
- 2 T. all-purpose flour
- ½ C. frozen chopped spinach, thawed and drained
- 1 T. fresh cilantro, chopped
- Salt and pepper to taste

PREPARATION

In a medium saucepan over medium heat, bring beer to a boil. Lower heat. Slowly stir in Monterey Jack cheese and flour. Cook and stir until cheese is melted, but not bubbly. Mix spinach, cilantro, salt, and pepper into the beer mixture. Serve warm with tortilla chips.

BEER CHEESE PRETZEL & DIP Makes 4 servings

INGREDIENTS

- ➢ 1 (16 oz.) package hot bread roll mix with yeast
- ➢ 1 C. shredded sharp cheddar cheese
- ➢ 1¼ C. beer
- ➢ 1 egg, beaten
- ➢ 2 T. kosher salt
- ➢ 1 (8 oz.) package cream cheese, diced and softened
- ➢ 1 (8 oz.) package processed cheese, cubed
- ➢ ¾ tsp. garlic powder
- ➢ ½ C. beer, room temperature

PREPARATION

Preheat oven to 350°. In a medium bowl, mix the hot bread roll mix with yeast and cheddar cheese. In a microwave or small saucepan, heat the 1¼ cup beer to almost boiling. Stir beer and egg into the flour mixture and knead for 5 minutes. Allow the dough to rest for 5 minutes, then roll into desired shape. Sprinkle with kosher salt. Bake 25 minutes in the preheated oven or until golden brown. In a food processor, blend the cream cheese, processed cheese, garlic powder, and warm beer. Refrigerate until serving with the baked dough.

SPICY PARTY PRETZELS Makes 15 servings

INGREDIENTS

- ➢ 1 C. vegetable oil
- ➢ 1 (1 oz.) envelope ranch dressing mix
- ➢ 1 tsp. garlic salt
- ➢ 1 tsp. cayenne pepper
- ➢ 1 (15 oz.) package mini twist pretzels

PREPARATION

Preheat oven to 350°. In a medium bowl, combine vegetable oil, ranch dressing mix, garlic salt, and cayenne pepper. Stir until well mixed. Place pretzels in an even layer on a jellyroll pan and pour vegetable oil mixture over pretzels. Stir until evenly coated. Bake for 1 hour, stirring occasionally to coat pretzels. Pretzels are done when toasted and crispy.

HOT BACON DRESSING Makes 2 ½ cups

INGREDIENTS
- 1 lb. bacon, diced
- ½ C. cider vinegar
- 2 tsp. dry mustard
- ½ C. diced onion
- 1 C. brown sugar
- 1 C. beer
- 2½ T. flour

PREPARATION
Fry bacon to a golden brown; remove from skillet and set aside. Leave scant covering of grease in bottom of skillet. Add vinegar, dry mustard, onion, and sugar and heat over medium heat. Combine beer and flour and add to skillet. Cook dressing until thickened, 6 to 8 minutes. Add reserved bacon pieces. Serve hot dressing over fresh spinach salad or mixed greens.

BBQ SAUCE Makes 3 ½ cups

INGREDIENTS
- 3 C. prepared BBQ sauce
- ¼ C. cider vinegar
- ¼ C. honey
- 2 tsp. onion powder
- 2 tsp. garlic powder
- Dash of hot pepper sauce

PREPARATION
In a medium bowl, whisk together BBQ sauce, vinegar, honey, onion powder, garlic powder, and hot pepper sauce until well mixed.

CAROLINA BBQ SAUCE Makes 2 ½ cups

INGREDIENTS

- 1 ½ C. prepared mustard
- ½ C. packed brown sugar
- ¾ C. cider vinegar
- ½ C. beer
- 1 T. chili powder
- 1 tsp. freshly ground black pepper
- 1 tsp. freshly ground white pepper
- ½ tsp. ground cayenne pepper
- 1 ½ tsp. Worcestershire sauce
- 2 T. butter, room temperature
- 1 ½ tsp. liquid smoke flavoring
- 1 tsp. hot sauce

PREPARATION

In a heavy, nonreactive saucepan, combine mustard, brown sugar, vinegar, and beer. Season with chili powder and black, white, and cayenne peppers. Bring to a simmer over medium-high heat. Do not boil, or the sugar and peppers will be scorched. Reduce heat and simmer for about 20 minutes. Mix in the Worcestershire sauce, butter, and liquid smoke. Simmer for another 15 or 20 minutes. Add a few dashes of the hot sauce to taste. Pour into an airtight jar and refrigerate overnight to allow flavors to blend.

★★★★ MAN CAVE FILM FEST ★★★★

TOP 10 COMEDIES

Nothing is more subjective than comedy. And, since we used our mulligan on the Top 16 Guy Movies, we'll have to keep this to a Top 10 and take a stand. (Yeah, we know, *Ghostbusters* and *This Is Spinal Tap* were left out…)

- *Groundhog Day*
- *Caddy Shack*
- *Young Frankenstein*
- *Animal House*
- *The Big Lebowski*
- *Blazing Saddles*
- *Anchorman*
- *Monty Python and the Holy Grail*
- *Airplane*
- *Midnight Run*

HONEY PECAN CHEX MIX Makes 18 servings

INGREDIENTS
- 7 C. Crispix cereal
- 1 C. mini twist pretzels
- 1 C. pecan halves
- ¼ C. butter
- ¾ C. brown sugar
- ¼ C. honey
- 1 tsp. vanilla

PREPARATION
Preheat oven to 250°. Lightly grease a 9" x 13" baking dish. Combine Crispix cereal, pretzels, and pecan halves in prepared baking dish. Mix until evenly incorporated; set aside. In a medium saucepan over medium heat, combine butter, brown sugar, and honey. Bring mixture to a boil, stirring frequently. Let mixture boil for 5 minutes without stirring. Remove from heat and stir in vanilla. Pour mixture over cereal mixture in baking dish. Toss until evenly coated. Bake for 1 hour, stirring every 15 minutes. Let mixture cool in baking dish. Store in an airtight container.

PEANUT BUTTER BLONDIES Makes 24 servings

INGREDIENTS
- 3 C. plus 2 T. flour
- ½ tsp. baking powder
- 1 tsp. baking soda
- ½ tsp. salt
- 1 tsp. cinnamon, optional
- 1 C. butter
- 2⅓ C. brown sugar
- 3 eggs
- 2 tsp. vanilla
- 3 C. peanut butter chips
- 1 C. chopped pecans, toasted*

PREPARATION
Preheat oven to 350°. Grease and flour a 9" x 13" baking dish and set aside. In a medium bowl, sift flour, baking power, baking soda, salt, and cinnamon; set aside. In a large saucepan over low heat, melt butter. Stir in brown sugar, mixing until completely dissolved; remove from heat and let mixture cool. Mix in eggs, one at a time, beating well after each addition. Mix in vanilla. Gradually add sifted dry ingredients, a little at a time, mixing until just blended. Fold in peanut butter chips and toasted pecans. Spread batter evenly in prepared pan. Bake for 30 to 35 minutes. Let cool before cutting into bars.

To toast, place chopped pecans in a single layer on a baking sheet. Bake at 350° for approximately 10 minutes or until pecans are golden brown.

BEER & PRETZEL CHOCOLATE PIE Makes 1 pie

INGREDIENTS
- 1 C. crushed pretzels
- ½ C. sugar
- ⅓ C. butter, melted
- 1 (3¼ oz.) package cook-and-serve chocolate pie filling
- 1 C. evaporated milk
- 1 C. beer
- Whipped topping

PREPARATION
Prepare crust by combining pretzel crumbs, sugar, and butter; blend well. Press into 9" pie plate and bake at 400° for 10 minutes. Set aside to cool. In saucepan, combine chocolate pie filling, milk, and beer; cook over medium heat until mixture comes to a rolling boil. Remove from heat, stirring occasionally for 5 to 10 minutes. Pour into pie crust and chill in refrigerator. Just before serving, spread whipped topping on top.

VANILLA BEER CAKE Makes 1 cake

INGREDIENTS
- 1 (18½ oz.) package yellow cake mix
- 1 (3½ oz.) package instant vanilla pudding mix
- 1 C. beer
- ¼ C. vegetable oil
- 4 eggs

PREPARATION
Preheat oven to 350°. Grease and flour a 10" Bundt pan. Combine cake mix and pudding mix in a large bowl. Add beer and vegetable oil and mix lightly. Add 4 eggs. Beat at high speed until mixture is thick, creamy, and smooth. Pour into a greased and floured Bundt pan. Bake for 55 minutes. Cool in pan for 10 minutes, then turn out onto a wire rack and cool completely. Frost as desired.

APPLE CRUMB CAKE Makes 1 cake

INGREDIENTS

- 2 C. sifted flour
- 1 C. brown sugar, packed
- ½ C. quick cooking oats
- ¾ C. butter or margarine, melted
- 1 C. sugar
- 3 T. cornstarch
- 1 C. beer
- 1 tsp. vanilla
- 6 medium apples, peeled and cored

PREPARATION

Mix flour, brown sugar, oats, and melted butter together until crumbs form. Place half of the crumbs in bottom of 13" x 9" x 2" cake pan. In a saucepan, mix sugar, cornstarch, and beer. Cook until thickened, stirring constantly; add vanilla. Thinly slice peeled apples and add to mixture, gently stirring to get all apple pieces coated. Spread apple mixture over crumb layer and sprinkle remaining crumb mixture on top, gently pressing down. Bake for 50 to 55 minutes at 350°.

BAKED APPLES Makes 4 baked apples

INGREDIENTS

- 4 large cooking apples
- ½ C. brown sugar
- ½ C. sugar
- 1 C. beer
- 1 T. margarine
- ½ tsp. cinnamon
- 2 to 3 drops red food coloring

PREPARATION

Core apples and peel about one-third down from top. Arrange, peeled side up, in an ungreased cake pan. In saucepan, mix brown and white sugars, beer, margarine, cinnamon, and food coloring. Bring to boil and continue boiling for about 5 minutes to form syrup. Pour over apples and bake uncovered for 1 hour. Serve hot or cold topped with whipped cream or ice cream.

MAN CAVE TIP

POKER

Poker should be fun, not intimidating. It should be a chance to spend time with buddies and family without any pressure beyond losing a couple of dough-dogs. There's no need to make the "rules" of the table stressful. You want Vegas, go to Vegas. A true Man Cave zone is zero pressure, 100% chill. That said, here are some things to remember when you're dealing a hand.

GO TO YOUR "HAPPY PLACE."
Poker will not erase a bad or depressed mood, and you need to play rationally. If your mind's not on the game, your fellow sharks will smell it like blood in the water. If you're in a bad mood, or get into one while playing, get some air.

DON'T BE AFRAID TO FOLD.
Bad song, good advice. You don't have to play every hand. The reason why beginners lose too often is they play way too many hands.

TRY TO STAY RELATIVELY SOBER.
Enough said. It's hard to play Five-Card Stud with ten cards in your hand.

KEEP YOUR EYES OPEN.
There are a lot of moving parts in poker. Along with the rules and etiquette, it's tough enough to remember what's in your own hand. But take a look around. Is there a straight or flush brewing? How's the flop fit? What's showing and what's folded? Keep your eyes on the cards.

DON'T BLUFF JUST FOR THE SAKE OF BLUFFING. Unless you're the Yankees, you can't win by throwing money at things. This is another rookie mistake. You don't have to stay in because you've got money in the pot. If you can't improve your hand, get out of Dodge. It's better to not bluff at all.

DON'T CALL TO KEEP SOMEONE HONEST. Why give away more money just to see what a player's hand is? If you feel you're beat, walk away and save the cash for another hand.

KEEP YOUR EYES OPEN, PART II: WATCH THE OTHER PLAYERS.
You've folded and you're nursing a beer. The best thing to do? Watch your opponents. Is there a tell when they bluff? Is there any pattern to how they fold or raise? Channel your inner Columbo and see who's guilty.

BABE RUTH BARS Makes 18 servings

INGREDIENTS

- 1 C. peanut butter
- 1 C. light corn syrup
- ½ C. brown sugar
- ½ C. sugar
- 6 C. cornflake cereal
- 1 C. chocolate chips
- ⅔ C. peanuts

PREPARATION

In a large saucepan over medium heat, combine peanut butter, corn syrup, and brown and white sugars. Cook, stirring occasionally, until smooth. Remove from heat and immediately stir in cereal, chocolate chips, and peanuts, mixing until evenly coated. Press mixture evenly in a greased 9" x 13" dish. Let cool before cutting into bars.

RASPBERRY OATMEAL BARS Makes 16 servings

INGREDIENTS

- ½ C. brown sugar
- 1 C. flour
- ¼ tsp. baking soda
- ⅛ tsp. salt
- 1 C. old-fashioned oats
- ½ C. butter, softened
- ¾ C. seedless raspberry jam

PREPARATION

Preheat oven to 350°. Grease an 8" square baking dish and line with aluminum foil; set aside. In a medium bowl, combine brown sugar, flour, baking soda, salt, and old-fashioned oats. Using a pastry blender, cut in softened butter until mixture is crumbly. Press 2 cups of the crumb mixture in the bottom of prepared pan. Spread raspberry jam over crumb layer to within ¼" of the edge of the pan. Sprinkle remaining crumb mixture over top of jam layer and press down lightly. Bake for 35 to 40 minutes, until bars are lightly browned. Let cool before cutting into bars.

BLOODY MARY Makes 2 servings

INGREDIENTS

- ¾ C. tomato juice
- 2 oz. vodka
- 1 to 2 dashes Tabasco sauce
- 1 tsp. lime juice
- Dash of Worcestershire sauce
- 1 tsp. prepared horseradish
- ¼ tsp. lemon pepper
- ⅛ tsp. Creole seasoning or salt
- ⅛ tsp. pepper
- Ice
- 2 long celery stalks

PREPARATION

In a pitcher, combine tomato juice and vodka. Mix well and stir in Tabasco sauce, lime juice, Worestershire sauce, prepared horseradish, lemon pepper, Creole seasoning, and pepper. Place ice in two tall glasses and pour Bloody Mary mixture over ice in glasses. Garnish each glass with a long celery stem.

SPIKED HOT CHOCOLATE Makes 1 serving

INGREDIENTS

- 1 C. prepared hot chocolate
- 1 T. chocolate syrup
- 2 oz. chocolate liqueur
- 1 T. whipped topping

PREPARATION

Fill a mug with prepared hot chocolate and stir in chocolate syrup and chocolate liqueur. Mix well. Garnish with whipped topping.

★★★★ MAN CAVE TIDBIT ★★★★

MAKING DRINKS IN BATCHES

Don't want to be chained to the bar mixing cocktails one at a time? Make a large batch of your favorite libation ahead of time. Grab some pitchers or carafes, fill them with manhattan, martini, or margarita mixtures and chill. When guests arrive, shake or stir the mixtures over ice, and pour. A good sangria or a Jack Daniels Down Home Punch will also do the trick.

SCREWDRIVER Makes 1 serving

INGREDIENTS
- Ice
- 1½ oz. vodka
- 3 T. orange juice

PREPARATION
Fill a cocktail shaker with ice and add vodka and orange juice. Shake until well mixed. Strain cocktail into glass.

HOT RUM CIDER Makes 3 ½ gallons

INGREDIENTS
- 1 (1.75 liter) bottle spiced rum
- 3 gallons apple cider
- Ground cinnamon to taste
- Ground nutmeg to taste
- 12 cinnamon sticks
- Whipped topping

PREPARATION
In a large jug, combine rum, cider, cinnamon, nutmeg, and cinnamon sticks. Mix well and let set overnight. To serve, stir until well mixed and heat in a large metal pot over grill, being careful not to boil. Ladle cider into mugs and garnish with whipped topping.

IRISH COFFEE Makes 1 serving

INGREDIENTS
- 2 tsp. sugar
- 1½ oz. Irish whiskey
- 1 C. hot brewed coffee
- 1 T. whipped topping

PREPARATION
In a mug, combine sugar and whiskey, stirring until sugar is completely dissolved. Stir in coffee and mix well. Garnish with whipped topping.

Index

ALPHABETICAL

ACQUISITION EDITOR:

Kerri Landis

ASSISTANT EDITORS:

Heather Stauffer and Katie Weeber

EDITOR:

Paul McGahren

COVER AND LAYOUT DESIGNER:

Jason Deller

PROOFREADER:

Lynda Jo Runkle